The Birds and the Beasts Were There

By KEN KRAFT

Just as some people are accident prone, author Ken Kraft is animal prone. Living all over the country, from the nation's capital to Pebble Beach, he has yet to escape the fringe members of our society: the irrepressible pet dogs, cats, raccoons, and the like who have conspired to make his world a topsy-turvy arena of confusion.

The conspirators have been varied— canaries, a baby crocodile, guinea pigs, mice, a drunken cat, an over-possessive Doberman—and their plots have been ingenious: the kleptomaniac dog who nearly succeeded in having Ken arrested for larceny, and the college mutt who all but kept him from pledging a fraternity and finally attacked his date, the campus queen.

Ken's only defense has been an unbridled sense of humor which is hilariously evident in this recollection of endlessly zany mishaps. Cleverly illustrated by David Pascal, this book presents a wholesome, laugh-packed picture of man at the mercy of his not-so-dumb animal friends.

Also by Ken Kraft:

LAND OF MILK & OMELETS

THE
BIRDS
AND THE
BEASTS
WERE
THERE

BY KEN KRAFT

ILLUSTRATED BY DAVID PASCAL

DOUBLEDAY & COMPANY, INC.

GARDEN CITY, NEW YORK

1961

This book is for Jim and Mark Saunders, whose friendship and understanding helped get it written, and who like animals too.

A WORD TO THE ANIMAL-WISE

If animal haters like this book, they'll have to blame the animals for it. I certainly don't hate animals (or birds, or fish, or reptiles—for there are some of them in here too). I have liked almost all of them I knew, and it wasn't until I started making notes that I came face to face with a gloomy discovery: All my life I seem to have been a patsy for these pets. Maybe some were fond of me in their way, and I know some weren't because they left scars to keep me reminded, but nearly all expected me to make life soft for them. Geography had nothing to do with it, either. In St. Louis when I was growing up I was having merely the first tastes of animal trouble that kept right on dogging me on the campus of the University of Missouri, in wartime Washington, in the Ozark Mountains, on a farm, along a Mississippi bayou. . . . Even at this moment, out here on the Pacific coast, a California dachshund named Hijack to whom I have given a home in his mature years is muttering because I would rather he gummed a ripe bone on the grass than on my lap.

So the facts will have to speak for themselves, helter-skelter and unscientific as they are. After all, science was the last thing I had in mind the time I got set to borrow a cocker spaniel for chasing squirrels out of pecan trees and got instead a muscular lion dog that chased a Bible salesman. Nor did science keep me out of trouble with an alligator living in my father's wine cellar. It also seems unscientific to me that a boy should have been presented with a bundle from heaven when he was counting on a coyote from Oklahoma. These are the sort of things that lead to trouble.

—Ken Kraft
Del Monte, California

CONTENTS

CONTENTS

THE BIRDS AND THE BEASTS WERE THERE

1

THE UNCLE DOG

YOU OUGHT TO GET STARTED ON DOGS," MY Uncle Dave said one day. "By the time I was your age I'd already had half a dozen." My age was nine, and Dave was twenty-two and my hero. If he said I needed a dog, I needed a dog.

"I think so too," I said. "As soon as he's in a good humor I'll ask Dad."

"Take it easy," Dave said. "You got to use your head. Has he ever told you you *couldn't* have a dog?"

"I never asked him."

"Good," Dave said. "Don't." He winked. "If you don't know how he feels about dogs, he can't kick if I get you one."

"I know how he feels about Spotty Boy next door," I said. "He hates him."

"That doesn't count," Dave said. "Why does he hate him?"

I explained that Spotty Boy, a large hairy mixture, kept sneaking into our yard and raiding the garbage cans—ours and that of the upstairs tenants of our flat on Garfield Avenue, in the west end of St. Louis.

"Ha! Your dog'll stop that pretty quick," Dave said. "I'll get you a good tough one." I felt it was as good as done. Dave was a pretty tough one himself. He was in the building trade, and besides being the handsomest man I knew, he was handy with his fists. When he was a boy he had once beaten up all the males in the seventh grade of Arlington School, one at a time, after they had ganged up on him following his transfer there. He was a great favorite with my mother, though Father had reservations.

Dave's dog did not appear for several days following our chat, and I was cloudy as to just where the dog was coming from. He was coming from an alley somewhere in south St. Louis, it turned out. This was happenchance and another demonstration of Dave's homemade code of ethics. He felt it was wrong to entice a dog with a collar on, but this one had none. It was a bull terrier, and when Dave spotted him sauntering down the alley, he opened his car door and invited him to take a spin. The dog accepted and that was that. The illegal climate of the seizure probably put a curse on me, for animals and trouble have arrived arm in arm at my door ever since.

Dave delivered the bull terrier that evening—a Friday—under cover of darkness. We were finishing dinner in the dining room, which was in the middle of the house between parlor and kitchen. My father was loading his pipe with cigar scraps and telling Mother what had happened at the office that day, when there was a disturbance at the kitchen door. Craning his neck, Father saw the door opening slowly, and he grew rigid. Our neighborhood was respectable but it had moments of misdemeanor. Father half rose, gripping his pipe as if he was thinking of shooting it, but a large and familiar hawk nose showed briefly in the partly open kitchen doorway.

"Why, it's just Dave," Mother said as the rest of the head appeared, smiling mysteriously. "Come in, Dave."

Without replying, Dave bent down. He was, we shortly found out, untying a length of sash cord he had fastened around the bull terrier's neck to persuade him along. It was an ill-advised move. The bull terrier was regretting his rashness in teaming up with Dave, and when he found himself free he started to leave.

There was a short and violent scuffle on our back porch and the splintering sound of a banister strut breaking. Directly over our heads we could hear our tenants scraping back their dining-room chairs and rushing toward their own back porch above ours. They were quiet people named Dixon with two rather mousy grown daughters, and my father approved of them because they paid the rent on the dot and were satisfied with the wallpaper.

As they charged out onto their back porch, Dave gained the upper hand, blocking the bull terrier's escape route with one leg and kicking our kitchen door all the way open with his other foot. With a smart lick of his open hand he sent the dog into the house. "Get along, you bugger!" he roared into the night air. "Goddammit anyway!"

The bull terrier passed through the kitchen like a bullet, and Dave sprang in behind him, victoriously slamming the kitchen door shut with a bang that shook the house. My father hopped to his feet and stood straddle-legged as if to catch the dog, his pipe still aimed, but the bull terrier flew straight down the hallway that led from kitchen to the front door. The door was closed, though, and he whipped left into the parlor where he got excellent traction on our best rug and came surging through the wide doorway into the dining room, zipping between Father's spread-out legs from behind and upsetting him. Father banged to the floor, swearing, Mother screamed as the dog passed her, and Dave, in ambush in the back hall, pounced. "*Got him,*" he bawled. Chuckling, he trotted into the dining room, the dog twisting savagely in his arms.

Mother retired behind her chair, and my father arose from the rug, thwacking cigar scraps from his vest front, and pulled out his watch to see if it was still running. I took the short cut under the table to meet my dog.

"Ain't he a dandy?" said Dave. He had a kind of half nelson on the dog, a pure white animal with dangerous-looking

black eyes and a headful of teeth. Overhead the sober footsteps of the Dixons returning from their back-porch sprint
were heard, and my father glanced upward, chewing his lip.

"A dandy!" he said bitterly. "He's an outlaw. Where'd you
get that beast?"

Dave sidestepped it. "He's just a little strange yet. He'll be
all right when he realizes this is home."

"Home be damned," said Father. "He's a home wrecker.
He's going to get a lot stranger, and right now—out with him!"

The dog and I were taking stock of each other. I let him
smell my hand, my left one because I could spare it better.
He twitched his pointed ears, and I took it as a good sign.

"I went to a lot of trouble getting this dog for Ken," Dave
said rather gruffly. "You don't find a dog like this every day.
But if you're going to be small about it—"

"Wait a minute, Dave," my mother said. She addressed
Father: "Now, Ed, this is a nice-looking dog, and considering
all the trouble Dave went to—"

"Trouble!" my father exploded. "*We'll* have the trouble.
What if this brute bites somebody? What if he goes after the
Dixons?"

"He isn't going to bite anybody," Mother said with a flip of
her chin. "Dave wouldn't get that kind of a dog." She swept
out to the kitchen with a stack of plates. "Bring him out here,"
she ordered. "The poor thing's probably just hungry."

He certainly was. He cleaned up the scraps from dinner in
five or six seconds and followed them with half a loaf of bread
and a pint of milk. Father remained grimly alone in the dining
room trying to get some sense out of the evening paper and
listening to the Dixons shuffling around overhead. The three
of us dragged the bull terrier to the basement and used a
pair of Father's old pants to make a bed under the stairway
after replacing the sash cord around his neck and tying it to
the stairs so that if either of the elder Dixons or their daughters came down, nothing unpleasant would occur.

I then remembered that in the excitement of arrival an important item had been overlooked. "What's his name, Dave?" I asked.

"Why—uh—Ripper," Dave said. "Yeah—call him Ripper."

It was a masterpiece of naming, as we found out the following morning. Fortunately my father's office worked on Saturdays and he had already left.

I hurried down the basement steps before breakfast, but by the time I hit the third tread I knew something was terribly wrong. Ripper's rope was hanging loose, chewed in two, and the basement floor was thatched with bits of my father's pants plus remnants of beige-colored gabardine. My father's good raincoat, I realized with horror, had been hanging in the basement to dry after a recent shower. A chilling ripping sound came just then from the Dixon end of the basement, and I raced the rest of the way down, yelling for Ripper.

He was poised beneath the Dixon basement clothesline, getting ready for another spring. They were terribly clean people and washed in between as well as on Mondays. I caught my breath—already Ripper had sprung several times. From the clothesline some long cambric garments of the Dixon daughters, lacy with eyelet embroidery, were now much lacier and a good deal shorter. The cement floor was sprinkled with their fragments, a sample of which also hung from one of Ripper's gleaming fangs.

I flung myself at him with a howl of dismay that brought my mother hastening down the basement steps, drying her hands on her apron. At the bottom she slowed momentarily, wallowing through Father's pants and raincoat with an expression of vague panic, and then came face to face with the rape of the clothesline. She threw her apron over her face and screeched faintly.

I anchored Ripper by twining my arms around his muscular body, and waited. Mother was unpredictable in crises.

Abruptly she dropped the apron and listened for footsteps on the Dixon back stairs. There were none. "Take the beast up to the kitchen," she hissed.

I dragged him off by the bit of sash cord still around his neck, to his fierce disappointment, while Mother rapidly assessed the damage.

"Four dollars should cover it," she muttered as she joined the villain and me in the kitchen. She had brought along the tattered lingerie remains, and she sank into a kitchen chair with the bundle in her lap.

I thought of four dollars and swallowed hard. My current assets were about fifteen cents and I wouldn't get my hands on four dollars in a lump until my birthday, months away. If the Dixon daughters had to wait on me to restore their unmentionables, the girls were in for some drafty times. But to my relief Mother took the view that it was a household obligation. She got the house money from the pantry and counted it. "Only two dollars, sixty-nine cents. Oh, my. And the Dixons are so touchy. . . ." She didn't have to go on. We were both thinking of my father. If he lost his prize tenants over this, not to mention his pants and raincoat, life would be difficult. As we sat there we heard Mrs. Dixon start clomping down their back stairway to get the laundry, and my mother leaped to her feet. Stuffing the bundle of tatters into the kitchen wastebasket, she raced Mrs. Dixon to the basement.

After ten minutes of muffled conversation below, she returned, pink and breathing hard. "She accepted it," she reported. "She was a little snippy, but she admitted the things weren't brand-new." She sat down and poured herself a cup of coffee. "But now," she said heavily, "what in mercy's name are we to do with this destroying devil?"

"If we had a good strong chain to tie him with—"

"Well, we haven't," she said crossly. "Besides, I don't want a chain clanking around. I'd keep thinking the place was haunted." She sighed. "We'll have to keep him up here today.

If you're through eating, you can take out the garbage. And be careful."

Her warning referred to our peculiar garbage-pail arrangements. Father had been trying various devices to outwit Spotty Boy, such as hanging the pails on the fence, then tying the lids on with rope, and finally hiding them under a crate. Only the crate had foiled Spotty Boy, but Mother got splinters in her hands from it, and Father was afraid Mrs. Dixon might, too, and get blood poisoning or sue him. He was now trying out a plan of weighing down the pails with bricks, in the hope they would either keep the next-door dog from dumping the garbage or would brain him when he tried. Meanwhile you were apt to get a toe mashed if you were in a hurry and toppled the bricks.

"Now go clean up the basement," Mother said when I returned, unmashed, from the garbage expedition. I inquired about her plans for the shredded pants and raincoat. "Burn them in the furnace with the trash," she said. "We won't say anything to your father for the time being."

Nobody had to say anything to him. He was a tidy man with his clothing, and that evening he went to the basement right after dinner to get his raincoat and put it back in his closet. Ripper was back in the basement, since the Dixon clothesline was now empty and my father was out of raincoats. Mother and I waited nervously upstairs, and I decided to help her with the dishes for the sake of appearances. After a few minutes Father came back upstairs and looked in his closet in the back hall. Then he lighted a match and looked harder. "Anne," he called, "have you put my raincoat somewhere?"

Seeing that it was I who had put it somewhere, Mother was able to answer factually. "No," she said. She was meticulous about never lying, but this failing had caused her to develop a kind of conversational hopscotch for her own defense.

"Well, do you know where it is?" Father asked. The coat had cost eighteen dollars and was almost new.

Since the literal answer would have been "It went up in smoke," Mother tacked. "You left it in the basement," she stated.

"It isn't there now," he said. "Isn't in my closet either." These were mere facts and needed no reply. Instead, Mother took her hands out of the dishpan and looked at them. "This water," she said fretfully, "is awfully hard on my skin." She stuck out both hands at him. "Look how red they are."

"Yes, yes," Father said, "but I want to know where my good—"

"You didn't look," Mother said, keeping her hands thrust under his nose. "Married ten years and my hands already look like an old woman's. A lot you care."

"Put something on 'em," Father said. "They look about the same as usual to me."

Mother dropped her hands. "Well, I like that!" she said, and put them on her hips. "'Look about the same as usual.' You used to say I had the softest hands you ever held!" She put her nose in the air and marched to the bathroom where she kept her cold cream.

Father jerked out his pipe and rammed some cigar scraps into it. "I meant they look as *good* as usual," he said, raising his voice.

She did not reply. He walked to the bathroom door, which she had closed behind her. "They *always* look good," he said loudly. He listened. "Yes, they do," he said. "They do to me." She said something I couldn't hear, and he smiled and lighted his pipe.

"Will you get mad if I tell you something?" she said through the door.

He laughed between puffs on his pipe. "Of course not. Bet you splurged on some fancy new lotion."

"No," she said. "We burned up your raincoat."

There was a clatter on the hall floor. My mother opened the bathroom door. "B-b-b-b," my father said, *burned up—*

"Heavens," Mother said. "You bit your pipe stem right in two, Ed." She put her foot on some bits of glowing cigar scraps on the hall rug. "Come and sit down," she said, "and I'll tell you all about it. You promised not to get mad, remember."

Father numbly gathered his pipe off the floor and followed her into the dining room, where she detailed the case of the tattered raincoat. She also threw in his old pants for good measure, but didn't bother to mention the Dixon girls' underneathies, since that account was squared.

"That damn dog—" Father said, half rising in his chair when she finished.

"You promised you wouldn't get mad."

"Dammit to hell," Father said, thumping back down. "*I'm not mad*. But I'm getting rid of that dog. Tomorrow!"

Neither my mother nor I had had any hopes that Father would have been so mild. We were quite sure he wouldn't let me keep Ripper, but we had expected more fireworks. I said good-by to the dog the next morning and left for Sunday school, since Father planned to take him out and lose him while I was gone. Ripper was not a friendly dog and our acquaintance had been shot with trouble, but I was sorry to be parting with him and there was a lump in my throat when I left.

When I returned from Sunday school, Father was in the back yard hacking at some boards with his hatchet. He could do more with a hatchet than most men accomplished with a whole toolbox. He already had a three-by-four-foot structure framed up, and he looked mad as he whacked away.

"Making a doghouse," Mother said, and held her apron in front of her face to smother a peal of mirth.

Spotty Boy, it seemed, had again visited our garbage sometime during the night and had solved the riddle of the bricks.

He had feasted on delicious chicken bones in the Dixon pail, and Father had put in a rough ten minutes after breakfast clearing the back yard of scattered bone splinters, potato peelings, pea pods, and an unsuccessful dried-peach surprise. "That's what changed his mind about Ripper," Mother told me. "He's going to leash him to the doghouse back there to guard the garbage pails."

Since it was now noon, Mother called a halt to the construction. "I don't mind your working Sunday morning," she said to Father, "but you're making too much noise for Sunday afternoon." He was all done except for the roof.

"I'll finish it tomorrow after work," he said. "But if I had another half hour—"

"We're going to take a nice walk after we eat," she said. "Come and get cleaned up."

She wished to take a family stroll with Ripper, it turned out, to Father's chagrin. He was a tall, well-built man and knew it, and didn't care a bit about parading a dog on a length of soiled sash cord with a knot in the middle. It worked out nicely, though. On the way back, Spotty Boy noticed us and had the poor judgment to snarl at Ripper. The bull terrier lunged after him and dragged me ten feet, before Father, at my mother's screeched command, snatched us back. Father loved a fighter, and he patted Ripper for the first time, chuckling grimly. "He'll fix him," he said. "Damn garbage hound."

Ripper fixed him, all right. The bull terrier spent Sunday night in the basement again, whiling away the time chewing his rope in two once more. Mrs. Dixon was an early starter with her Monday wash, and this Monday she was extra early. My father, always the first up in our family, was in the bathroom starting to shave when our tenant reached the basement with her bag of laundry. When she saw Ripper ambling around, she wasted no time opening the outside door, and he emerged into the back yard.

Spotty Boy had jumped our alley gate and was just then nudging the garbage pail, and immediately all hell broke loose in the back yard. Father dropped his razor in the wash-basin and galloped out to the kitchen door, wearing his lather. He was just in time to see Spotty Boy tear himself loose and go howling over the gate, instantly followed by Ripper with a mouthful of shaggy hair. Father stood like a rock on the back porch while the sounds of flight and vengeance flew down the alley and faded away in the distance. He came back inside, his lather twitching.

"Your dog's gone, I'm afraid," he said to me as I tumbled out of my sofa bed in the dining room. Mother came hurrying from the bedroom in a wrapper, and he told what had hap-pened.

"He'll come back," Mother said. "Dave wouldn't pick out a tramp dog."

Ripper never did come back, however, and even Spotty Boy was gone for several days. When he did return, he was in such poor condition that it took him another week or so to work up enough nerve to tackle our garbage pails again. It did him no good whatever. Having no dog now to put in his unfinished doghouse, Father put the garbage pails in it in-stead, with a slant roof on top, and it worked like a charm. From the kitchen window we could see Spotty Boy inhaling through the doghouse door, but he couldn't push his way in-

side or lift the roof, which was hinged. My father was so
entertained that he waltzed out and bought himself a twenty-
dollar raincoat and a new imitation amber pipe stem, guar-
anteed accident-proof.

2

SEX AMONG THE COYOTES

Y CHILDHOOD WAS A RETARDED ONE IN SEXual awareness, by today's standards, and a bit poky even for those times. I was all of ten years old before I stumbled heavily over sex, tripped up by a coyote.

We were still in our Garfield Avenue flat, and I was nicely established in a tight union with four neighbor boys, all of us about the same age. Except for one, a buck-toothed youngster named Ed, we were free agents without younger kin to look after. Ed had a kid sister and had to stay home and mind her now and then, but since his father owned a grocery store and was a valuable source of empty boxes, we forgave him. We had no interest at all in girls and especially none in little sisters. Our whole curiosity about sex orbited mildly around a single mystery: Where did babies come from?

Ed had been told the doctor brought them. Another member, Kirk, was informed they were usually found under cabbage leaves. The rest of us had had our questioning cut short with the story of the stork. We felt the stories canceled each other out, and as a matter of fact we had more important things to think of. Summer vacation was approaching, and we were building a clubhouse.

We were building it out of Ed's father's grocery boxes, having established squatters' rights on a vacant lot beside the grocery store. Using the boxes as building blocks, we had run up a functional dwelling, six feet by eight, with a wealth of cupboard space since the boxes faced inward. We were now accumulating boards for a roof, and the result was becoming so impressive that a sobering thought came. Kirk was the first to voice it. He was the club's most practical mind.

"How about when we aren't here?" he asked. "What if somebody busts in and gets our stuff?" We were caching dried corn silk and tissue paper for cigarettes; an old but useful deck of "Rook"; a mildewed history of the St. Louis Fire Department; and a collection of streetcar transfers and magazine ads of motorcycles. Also a few potatoes to be baked someday in a campfire.

"We'll just snap a lock on the door," Ed said. "I can get one off my father." But Kirk snorted. Our construction could not keep out any prowler able to lift a foot and kick.

"What we need," Kirk said after a few more moments' thought, "is a good watchdog to stay here on guard." It seemed a brilliant stroke, but none of us had a watchdog. Since Ripper had left, my own home lacked dogs, and the families of the other boys opposed dogs on principle. However, having had one, I was voted the member most likely to succeed, and became a committee of one to look into it.

I waited until after dinner that evening to broach the subject with Father, timing it for when he was loading his pipe with cigar scraps. This was usually a mellow moment and I struck out with confidence, having rehearsed my speech. "I've been thinking, Dad," I said. "About vacation coming and everything, and it seems to me this would be a pretty good time to do some things."

I paused, and my father, studying a row of figures on a piece of scratch paper beside his plate, glanced up briefly. "You're too young to get a summer job," he said.

He returned to his figuring while I wondered how on earth he had got off on such a tangent. I had no desire for a sum-

mer job aside from mowing my grandfather's lawn. My grandparents lived only half a block away, on Union Avenue, and I had the inside track on this profitable chore.

"I didn't mean a job," I said. "Anyway, I'll be pretty busy. I got a lot of things to do this summer, and—"

"So have I," said my father, rather sharply. He broke his pencil point and swore under his breath. "Your mother and I will *both* be pretty busy this summer." He changed pencils and frowned at his figures, which seemed to deal with money matters. "I wouldn't be surprised," he said, "if you found yourself a little busier around here too."

He was about to say something else, but my mother came in from the kitchen just then and a look passed between them. "That's all right, Anne," my father said. "I didn't say anything."

It seemed to me he had, but adults had their own language. Besides, my mother had been snappish lately, and Father was watching his step. She had bought quite a few new dresses that spring, and not only had he paid the department-store bills without reading them off to her, but he kept assuring her she looked fine.

At any rate it was plain I had picked a poor time to talk about getting a dog. I postponed it and took a walk up the street to my grandparents' house to see how soon the lawn could stand a mowing. I thought, too, that I might sound out my grandmother on a dog deal. Nothing pleased her more than some undercover plotting. But here, too, I ran into complications. My grandmother was suddenly getting ready to take a trip and was sorting out her wardrobe. It was impossible to talk to her sensibly. She was going off to visit a daughter-in-law's family in southern Oklahoma for six weeks. She scarcely knew these folks but she got on easily and was intrigued by the fact that they lived on a farm. She wanted to live on one herself, but my grandfather wouldn't hear of it.

She kept a rotogravure picture of a Jersey cow framed on the kitchen wall, for compensation, I suppose.

Two days after that, my grandfather took her to Union Station to catch the train, and I went along to help with the luggage. When she traveled, my grandmother took care of the overflow with paper bags, and she had eight or nine of them this time, some with gifts for her hosts and one with a snack of lunch for herself, aggravating my grandfather who was neat and traveled in style. But helping with the bags did enable me to mention my dog problem to my grandmother again at the last minute, and it had more effect than I thought at the time. I had doubted that she even knew what I was saying; she had a fixation whenever she went anywhere that Grandfather was putting her on the wrong train and she would end up in New York.

But two weeks later she sent me a letter. It had a genuine Oklahoma postmark, and contained a thrilling, if veiled, promise. "Having fine time on farm," she wrote in her immense and scrawling handwriting. "You would like it fine here feeding hogs. No extra dugs but lots kyots."

She signed it "Danno," the name we grandchildren called her, but I needed no signature. "Dugs" I knew meant "dogs," for she spelled by guess, and "kyots" I finally interpreted as "coyotes." It had never occurred to me to try for anything except a dog. But if dogs were scarce in Oklahoma and coyotes were plentiful—! I shot off a letter to my grandmother by the next day's mail.

I said I was glad she was having a good time and that we were all well, though Dr. Henckler, our family physician, had dropped by twice to see my mother, who seemed healthy enough to me. I then got down to business and asked her to tell me more about the coyotes, which I had hurriedly looked up in *A Natural History for Boys,* a reference work which had seemed academic till then. From it I got the impression a coyote was a sort of family-sized wolf. On second thought I added a postscript saying I thought it would be well to get a puppy coyote so I could train it from the start.

My grandmother's reply, a couple of weeks later, required some decoding. "Kiled hog today," she wrote. "Big church tomorrow, all going. How is everybody is it hot there. Kyots howled last nit." As I made it out, the remark about howling coyotes was the key. It sounded as if they had caught some, for I knew that dogs howled when tied up. And since a hog had been killed, it was probably for the big church something, a community celebration to mark the capture.

If this deduction seems farfetched, let me say that everybody had to read my grandmother's letters in such a manner. She wrote as if she were talking fast, making one word do for twenty and shrugging and winking as she went, and you had to read these meanings into the letter. She had once given one of her daughters a terrible turn by sending her a postcard saying: "Bad weather here. Pop dying. Send flowers." All that she meant was that my grandfather was fretting over a rainy spell as usual because he was longing to play golf, and she was reminding her daughter to mail some home-grown aster seed she had promised.

Since things now seemed to be going forward briskly in Oklahoma, I felt safe in letting my playmates in on the secret. None of them had made the slightest progress toward getting a club watchdog, let alone a coyote, and they were dazzled.

"What do you say we call this *The Coyote Club?*" Kirk proposed, and it was carried by acclamation. Emmett, another member, who usually got E for excellence in school art class, volunteered to create a club coat of arms for the door, and borrowed my natural history book to see what a coyote looked like. I could not have made more stir if I had arranged for a dragon. I resolved to do something nice for my grandmother when she got home.

For the time being, I said nothing to my parents about the coyote. I was not sure how my father would take it, and it seemed better to present him with a *fait accompli*. He never did have much luck opposing my grandmother, his mother-in-law. And Mother appeared too much immersed in affairs of her own to listen calmly to plans for welcoming a coyote.

I wrote my grandmother again, praising her to the skies, and said that if she wanted to bring a couple of coyote pups that would be fine, since it had occurred to me that I could keep one at home and one at the clubhouse. She did not answer but I was not surprised. Two letters per trip were over par for her and anyway her visit was nearly over.

As a matter of fact, she cut it short by several days. This was amazing. Usually she stayed longer than she had planned, and she was enjoying Oklahoma. My father was the one who told me she was arriving. It was a Friday and he got home from work early in the afternoon, also an unusual thing. He met me at the door as I returned from school, and told me to go to my grandmother's for dinner. "And you can stay all night," he said hurriedly, handing out my pajamas and toothbrush. "Get right along, now. Grandmother's getting home today."

I started to ask if he and my mother were coming, too, but I thought of the coyote, or coyotes, and decided to let well enough alone.

I ran all the way, but my grandmother was not there yet. She was coming on an evening train, said my Aunt Stella, who was looking after Grandfather and the house. She gave me a searching look, and I wondered if she had got wind of the coyote.

Dinner was quiet without Grandmother's chatty presence and also because Grandfather was hard of hearing, which made conversation across the big table strenuous. I expected to go to Union Station with him afterwards to meet the train, but he abruptly handed me a dollar bill and told me to see a movie and keep the change. When I got back from it, only Stella was there and she suggested so strongly that I go to bed that I did, intending to stay awake till I heard Grandmother and my coyote arrive.

I went to sleep anyway and it was just as well. My grandmother didn't get home until nearly breakfast time the next morning, though Grandfather had been home most of the night, I found. What woke me up was my grandmother's voice. She was speaking to Grandfather, who was in the bathroom shaving.

"A boy, Pop," she said.

"Hey?" Grandfather said. "Speak up."

"A *boy*," Grandmother yelled. "Another boy."

My coyotes! I thought, scrambling out of my bed in the spare room. I rushed into the hall and down to the bathroom. My grandfather, razor poised, looked down and grinned at me, and Grandmother kissed me. She looked tired but contented. "Can I see him, Danno?" I asked, thinking she must have one there with her, though I didn't think my grandfather would be partial to coyotes in the bathroom.

"You can see him pretty soon," she said.

"Where are you keeping him?" I asked, and she looked amused.

"Why," she said, "he's at home. At your home."

A small chill took hold of me. Something here, I felt, was not at all right. And when my grandfather asked, "How is Anne?" and Grandmother said she was doing fine, thank the Lord, I was almost sure of it. But then Grandmother beckoned mysteriously toward her room down the hall.

"I've brought you something," she said. "Come."

My hopes bounced up again. In her room she sorted over a new batch of paper bags she had come home with, and handed me one. Though it seemed a peculiar way to ship a coyote pup, the bag had a squashy feel and smelled right, rather wild. I decided I could be happy even with only one coyote, and when I reached in I felt fur. I drew the thing out and then stood staring at what I held. My grandmother waited but there was nothing I wanted to say.

"It's a rabbit skin," she said. "I thought of you and got one of the boys to skin one for me when they went hunting. Isn't it fine?"

I nodded dumbly.

"You can do something with it," she said. "Boys can always think of something."

I gulped. "Danno," I said hoarsely, *what's* at home? That I can see pretty soon?"

She chuckled. "Why, a new baby brother. A fine eight-pound baby brother. He came last night."

It was nearly the end of me in The Coyote Club. Emmett already had the coat of arms made, painted on a wooden shield ready to fasten to the door, and he took it hard. Everybody felt I had let the club down disgracefully, and so did I. I could see that in a few years I would even be inflicting them with my kid brother tagging along behind. It was humiliating, but, as they all finally admitted, it was life. It had to be borne.

After some discussion we fastened Emmett's coyote coat of arms to the clubhouse door anyway since it was all finished, in brilliant blues and reds with crossed swords and the head of a coyote, fangs bared, in profile. Just below it we tacked the rabbit skin to the door also, and when we admitted new members later on we told them the pelt was that of a fierce dwarf coyote, seized in an Oklahoma jungle by a patron of the club.

3

CANARIES IN THE BEDROOM

"I'LL NEVER BE RICH," MY FATHER ONCE RE-
marked in his middle years. "I won't be hard
up but I never could save money." He cer-
tainly never could. All his life, every time he made a start at
it some stock salesman would get hold of him. The next thing
my mother knew, Dad would come home with a spring in his
step and a folder full of booklets and fold-outs printed in
four colors on glossy paper, and they would argue all evening
across the dining-room table. My mother was for 3 per cent
government bonds.

"We've only got five hundred dollars, Anne," my father
would yell across the centerpiece. "That'd only be fifteen dollars a year interest. What can you do with fifteen dollars?"

"I can buy two everyday dresses with it," my mother would
say. "Maybe three, on sale."

This practical line of thought always gave my father
lumps. He thought in large, four-color terms. "With five hundred dollars," he said, "we can buy fifty shares of this stock.
Fifty. But we have to make up our minds right away. As
soon as it goes on the open market the price'll shoot up."

"What interest does it pay?" Mother asked.

"Stocks don't pay interest, Anne. They pay dividends."

"Then what dividends—"

"This is a growth stock," my father said quickly. Such
terms meant absolutely nothing to Mother.

"Why put our good money into it if it doesn't pay any-thing?" she demanded. "Government bonds . . ."

I never heard the end of these arguments, which went on long after I was in bed, but somehow my father always won. We never bought a single government bond except in war-time, but we owned shares in, from time to time, three empty mines—lead, silver, and diamond—were participants in an en-terprise which pounded bananas into an unsalable flour, and helped keep afloat a boring-tool concern which apparently was putting the money into sample holes it was boring. And there were others.

Perhaps it was because he grew tired of letting other peo-ple lose his money that my father decided one time to do something on his own. He chose birds, and the venture took my mother completely off guard.

"I was looking at some canaries today," Father said one evening at dinner.

"Canaries?" Mother repeated. Dad had never shown any interest in birds before and would not have crossed the street to see a dodo.

"Hartz Mountain rollers," he said casually.

"What's a roller?" Mother said, falling right into the trap. Father smiled, reached into his pocket, and drew forth a bright-colored booklet.

"Now wait—this isn't a prospectus," he said as my mother's eyes narrowed. "It's a very informative pamphlet on breed-ing."

"Breeding *canaries*, for heaven's sake?" Mother cried.

"Did you know you can get up to twenty dollars for a fine singer? Five singers—a hundred dollars. In one breeding you can recover your whole investment and more. In the first fis-cal year you should, conservatively speaking, realize three hundred per cent on your money."

"Who's going to pay this twenty dollars each?" Mother asked.

"They're in great demand," Father said. "I'll probably sell them direct and cut out the middleman's profit. Those are details I'll work out later, when I have the stationery printed."

"Just a minute," Mother said. "Where will you keep them?" We were then living in a small cottage on, by coincidence, Burd Avenue, a few blocks farther west than the old flat on Garfield. The cottage was too small for me to have a room of my own, and I slept on the Murphy-in-a-Door bed in the dining room.

"I'll keep them on the sleeping porch," my father said. "I've been thinking of glassing it in for a sunroom anyway. It'll add value to the house." The house had been on the market for a while. My father hoped to make his fortune in real estate, also. I was interested in seeing the house sold so I could get my own room in the next one. Ted, my little brother, was still too young to need one, and occupied a small bed in our parents' room.

Mother went along with glassing in the porch though she had no faith in canaries. She felt they were too small to count on and she was not sure they laid eggs.

Father had no doubt of it. As soon as the sunroom was glassed, he brought home two boxy things he called breeding cages. Then he brought home two more and made platform shelves for all of them on one wall. "All the canaries I've seen had nice brass cages," Mother said, frowning at them. She said she wasn't going to waste beauty on things like that, and she stopped plans to get flowered cretonne draperies for the sunroom. Father also had the bottom of the ex-porch boarded up, and the whole remodeling bill came to about $250. He said he'd charge the canaries with half and call the rest capital investment in the house. He bought a set of double-entry books for the canary business and a filing cabinet with cards to keep track of the matings. Then he stocked the four cages with one pair of birds each. There were grilles in the middle of the cages, and you removed them when the birds seemed in the mood for mating. Presently Father brought home some small mesh baskets. He had also added a cabinet to hold birdseed and other supplies, and the sunroom was getting crowded.

"Nests," he said when Mother stared at the baskets, and he produced a bag full of hair she had not noticed.

"Is that *hair?*" she cried. He nodded. "How do you know it's clean?" she asked, and he looked pained. "Well, it doesn't look any too clean to me," she said. "I could have given you all the hair you wanted, from my brushing."

"This is special hair," he said. "They won't lay eggs in ordinary hair." Before she could say what she thought of that, he asked for a small silver spoon, and she put her hands on her hips. "The spoon," he said patiently, "is to remove the eggs as they're laid, so the hen canary won't break any before she has a clutch and can start setting." She handed over a souvenir Louisiana Purchase Exposition spoon with a martyred air.

When one of the birds at length laid an egg, we were all surprised except Father. He put it in a cotton-lined cigar box in his supplies cabinet and marked up a ten-dollar credit for the canaries. "I thought they were worth twenty," Mother said. He explained that half the eggs would hatch females, relatively worthless. She took it a little personally, but he admitted the females might bring a dollar or so each and pay some of the overhead.

Pretty soon another of the canaries began laying. Father kept her eggs separate to keep his pedigree lines pure. The canaries did not lay eggs as often as chickens do, so it took a while to accumulate a clutch. He had three from Alice, the name he gave the first canary that laid, and two from Bonita, the second one. He was naming them alphabetically in the order that they began producing, for convenient reference. He had an orderly mind.

He was counting on a fourth egg to make a clutch from his original producer the day he got his first serious setback. Mother lingered in the kitchen when he got home, gave her a quick kiss, and hurried to the sunroom. He was there but a moment when we heard him bellow. Mother averted her head as he came rushing out holding two cotton-lined cigar boxes labeled with the proper names.

"Alice's eggs!" he shouted at Mother. "They're all gone! And there are *three* in Bonita's box!"

"Now, Ed," Mother said. "Please don't make a scene. The child didn't mean any harm."

"Child?" Father said wildly. He darted a glance at me, but he knew me too well to think I would have tarried unless I was innocent. His eyes traveled to my mother's skirt. Ted was hiding behind it. "*Him?*" Father cried. He blinked. "Why, he couldn't even reach the shelf!"

"I was tidying up the sunroom a little," Mother said, stirring gravy. She glanced over her shoulder at Father. "If you're going to harbor a flock of messy birds—"

"How could he get at the *eggs?*" Father demanded like thunder.

"I laid the boxes on a chair while I was cleaning the cabinet shelves. Dust! My land, you could write—"

"On a chair!" Father said in a croak.

"He only dropped two of them, for heaven's sake," Mother said. "And I was the one who had to clean them off the floor, not you."

"Do you know which two?" Father asked after a few moments, but his tone was without hope. Mother didn't have the faintest idea. She had cornered the remaining eggs,

which were rolling around the chair seat, and popped them
all into Bonita's box.

Father considered throwing them away and starting all
over, but he couldn't afford to be so particular now. The other
two hen canaries were not laying at all, and he had been
counting on sixteen eggs, $160 net, for his first hatch. He put
off having his business stationery printed and also deferred
the purchase of a high-class singer which he had been planning to get to teach the young males.

Canaries had diverted Father's mind from selling the
house, but about this time a prospect showed up and took
him by surprise. The negotiations that followed took me by
surprise, too, for the next thing I knew, our house was sold
and a builder was rushing one up for us in University City,
a suburb of St. Louis, on a lot Father had bought there one
time on speculation. So I was finally going to get a room of
my own and I should have been pleased. I was, but there was
a drawback. I had lately made friends with a new boy in the
neighborhood, Albert Binks, and I hated to lose him so soon.
He swore something awful, and I was studying him. At home
I had no such opportunities. "Dammit" was my father's
standard oath in moments of stress, and if goaded beyond
endurance the best he could do was "Dammit to hell." Lately
he had reached this point almost daily, but he sounded in-
sipid next to Albert.

Father continued to tend the birds, though in a more me-
chanical fashion, as the real estate arrangements progressed,
and we drove out to University City frequently so he could
keep an eye on the new house. The cost was running up and
he had lost all interest in putting any more money into canaries. Out of two clutches of eggs he had finally accumulated, only one egg had hatched and he was almost sure the
bird was a female. He stopped keeping records.

Our new house was getting a built-in sunroom since they were in style, and I took it for granted that the canaries were to go there. There was no place else that I could see, as building costs had shot too high to permit a guest room which the birds might have occupied. Besides the sunroom there was a living room, a dining room and kitchen downstairs, and upstairs were two bedrooms—a big one for my parents and Ted, and for me a sort of Z-shaped one which seemed as good as a castle after the fold-out bed in the dining room on Burd. I worked out the places where furniture could go when I had some, and promoted a picture of a moose for one wall and some of clipper ships for the others.

We moved in June, Father having arranged the schedule so that I finished the school term and the builder finished the house in a dead heat. The day we moved, my father took the canaries and drove ahead of the moving truck to show the way while Mother finished cleaning up the old house and I said good-by to my friends, especially Albert Binks. Albert showed his regret by swearing horribly at me, and Father came back for us at four o'clock.

He was perspiring freely and seemed tired, but there was an air of accomplishment about him. "All moved in," he told Mother. "Furniture all placed. I had a little trouble with Ken's room but I managed."

"What trouble?" I said, but he was going around closing windows and did not answer. All the way over to the new house he was too busy talking to Mother and trying to pass the Delmar streetcars for me to quiz him, and I decided he had probably had a little trouble getting my leather Morris chair through the doorway to my room. Mother had bought me a bed and dresser from a neighbor who had more furniture than she needed and she had thrown in the Morris chair when I became infatuated with it. When you pressed a button, the back tilted, producing a clubby feeling.

I saw the chair as soon as I entered the new house, but it

was not in my room upstairs. It was in the sunroom, looking
ill at ease. I sped up the stairway to my room, feeling I had
been swindled, and when I got to the doorway and looked in,
I could hardly speak. Father's canary supplies cabinet was
jammed against my new dresser on the west wall, his canary
filing cabinet was squeezed against my bed on the north wall.
And the south wall where the Morris chair was to have gone
was bristling with the canary breeding cages on brackets, the
canaries chirping busily and perfectly at home.

My parents came hurrying up the stairs, dragging Ted
along, and Father started to explain things in a brisk and
businesslike voice. I looked at him coldly but he had no
shame. "It'll be a nice hobby for you," he said. "Give you a
feeling of responsibility and make you some spending money
maybe. I'll buy the birdseed," he added quickly.

Mother, looking embarrassed at having been privy to this
outrage, said nothing and I was left stranded. They both
turned to go back downstairs and Father waved toward the
cages. "You may as well start right in," he said. "Give them
fresh feed and water and clean the cages before dinner."
They departed, leaving me with Ted and the canaries.

Although I had sometimes watched Father doing it, I had
never tended the canaries myself. However, I decided immediately to streamline the job to about five minutes instead of
the twenty it took him. I whisked out the papers in the cage
bottoms, sending the canaries into shrieks, and hurried to
the bathroom for a glass of water to fill all their cups at a
swoop. While there I heard my brother screeching with joy.
He was usually a solemn child. I returned with the brimming
glass, wondering what had pleased him, and a canary nearly
hit me in the eye on its way out of the room and down the
stairwell.

In the interest of efficiency I had changed all the cage papers at once, but somehow I had neglected to close the cage
doors again. Every canary had struck a blow for liberty, and

my new bedroom was thick with them zipping through the air and chirping shrilly as they charged the windowpanes and bounced off.

Subconsciously I still considered them Father's canaries and I should have been alarmed, but the injustice of the thing overwhelmed me. When a dropping from one flying canary suddenly smacked my new dresser and another spattered on the mattress of my new bed, I set the glass of water down and went after them.

"Get back in your cages, you little bastards!" I yelled. I had never used this ringing word out loud, but it and other of Albert Binks's repertoire surged into my head as the canaries zoomed about it.

I leaped at a bird beating its wings against a window, captured it and thrust it back into a cage. "And *stay* there, you perishing bitch!" I roared, slamming the cage door. Ted giggled hilariously, and I did not notice the clatter of my parents' feet ascending the stairway. I jumped into the air for a grab at another bird, Bonita, I think, and missed as she banked and sped out the doorway. "Oh, goddam your guts," I cried.

Bonita struck my father in the chest as he burst onto the top landing, his mouth open in horror at me. He snatched at her and missed too.

"*Young man*," he said in a terrible voice, "*what does this mean?*"

At the sight of him filling the doorway the enormity of my act abruptly hit me. He often clouted me for such things as getting home a little late and would stop my allowance if I grew careless about chores, but never had I done anything so awful as this. Nothing short of packing me off to military academy, I felt, could pay my debt to society now.

For the moment, though, the canaries diverted Father. Two more aimed for him and as he ducked they bulleted downstairs. "The windows!" he yelled. He whirled and raced

down after them, nearly bowling over Mother who was trying to see into my room over his shoulder.

She glanced at me, biting her lip, and I looked at the floor.
Downstairs we could hear Father galloping around, slamming down windows. As yet we had no screens up. He paused
at the bottom of the stairs and roared up: "Come down here
and help me catch these things, dammit!" I ran down, and
my mother followed, got a dish towel, and used it as a net.
Out of the nine birds we captured three, counting my catch
in the bedroom. The others got out the open windows and
away.

Father thrust the captives into cages and grimly returned
downstairs where the rest of us were waiting, still breathing
hard. I steadied my lower lip and prepared to go down
bravely.

Father faced me, his legs slightly parted and his fists
clenched. "Where did you ever pick up such filthy—" he began, but Mother stepped up.

"I'm glad, Ed," she said.

Father looked as if she had struck him.

"I mean I'm glad they got away," she said. "The poor things
deserve their freedom. Besides, I'm sick and tired of them."

Father wobbled his head as if it was coming loose and
leveled a prosecutor's finger at me, but Mother got between
us and folded her arms. "He was sorely tried, Ed," she said.
"And just remember, you use terrible language yourself. You
set the children a bad example." Father made noises in his
throat but none came out sensibly.

For several moments nobody spoke, and then Ted did,
quite plainly. "Lit-tle bas-tard," he said, and giggled, and my
father, his jaw muscles working, strode off to the basement
to unpack some trunks.

It took several weeks to break my brother of swearing. I
finally gave him one of the canaries to bribe him. It was the
one solitary bird that had hatched and it eventually outlived

the other two we had recaptured. Although it was a hen canary as my father had feared, it learned to sing in a fashion,
for its own amusement, by listening to the phonograph. After
the breeding cages were finally tossed into the attic, Mother
got the little hen canary a nice brass cage and put it in the
sunroom on display. She said it would be a good reminder
for my father next time he got an idea.

4

THE BREADLINE GUINEA PIGS

FTER MY FATHER GOT OVER HIS INDIGNATION toward me for using profanity on the canaries, he began to have a few twinges about the ethics of having dumped them on me. He didn't admit this, since he believed in looking forward in hope, not backward in error. However, he gave himself away by showing little leniencies toward me, and then he decided to make amends more definitely. He decided to get me some guinea pigs for pets.

The canaries were certainly no pets. They had no talent for anything but eating, and my mother was sure they were smelling up my room. She had to go by guess here, for her own sense of smell had been blunted by sinus trouble years before. This let her in for some awkward predicaments and at about this time she ran into a new one. It was shortly before my father got the guinea pigs, so no one could have foreseen the coincidence.

By moving into a new neighborhood we had lost all our old deliverymen. Most of the new ones—the milkman, laundryman, and such—were no novelty to Mother. The trouble began when a man arrived in a bakery truck.

In our old neighborhood there had been no such service. We patronized a bakery down the block, where Father bought coffee cake every Saturday noon on his way home. By then his office was working only half a day on Saturdays.

He always bought more coffee cake than we needed and then nagged everyone to help eat it up. Mother had to pay him for it out of her house money, so the oversupply had long been a sore point with her.

On his first appearance at our new home the young man driving the bakery truck came trotting up our driveway with a metal basket hung over one arm and knocked confidently at the back door. He told Mother he was Casey the bakery man and then waited expectantly. His basket of things smelled so good, they usually did the selling for him. But Mother, unable to detect anything short of ammonia or a shockingly strong cheese, was not swayed.

She said she guessed we could use a loaf of poppyseed bread. She always hated to say no to anyone selling something at the door.

Casey looked downcast. He had bread, of course—poppyseed, raisin, whole wheat, and Boston brown bread—but he could not understand this stony attitude toward his fancier goods. He hopefully lifted his basket cover a little more to let the fragrance out, but Mother paid no attention.

"Um-m-m! Doesn't it smell good, ma'am?" Casey cried with the energy of desperation, and Mother came to attention. She never let on to strangers that she couldn't smell anything. She hastily inhaled. "Oh, delicious," she said.

"Coffee cake," Casey said proudly. "One of our big specialties."

Mother peered at the stollens, crumb cakes, and jelly rolls, and her eyes lighted. "Well, well," she said. "This is Friday—I guess it'll keep. That pineapple stollen, please."

For dinner that evening she served the poppyseed bread and asked my father if he liked it. He made the mistake of saying it was fine. "Good," she said. "I bought coffee cake from the same bakery deliveryman, so don't get any tomorrow, please."

He stared at her for several seconds. "Deliveryman?" he said at last. "You know that I always buy the coffee cake at Schneider's."

"Well, I always pay for it," Mother said smoothly, "and the man has a nice selection. Furthermore, I won't have half of it left on my hands this week, going to waste. I only bought one."

Father left the table with silent dignity the moment he was through. He didn't buy any coffee cake the next day on his way home, and when Mother served Casey's special at Sunday breakfast he barely picked at it, though it was pretty good. "See?" Mother said. "One was plenty. And I saved at least sixty cents."

This order of things lasted for two more weeks, but the Saturday after that, Father brought home a caramel roll from the old bakery. "I just dropped in to tell them why I hadn't been by lately," he said when my mother put her hands on her hips. "They missed me." The clerks at the bakery were blond German girls who looked as if they spent their spare time scrubbing each other. They knew my father by name and saved out the best things for him. When he told Mother he wouldn't charge her for the caramel roll, she calmed down.

The next Saturday he brought a jelly roll and a dozen nut twists from Schneider's and ate so much of them at Sunday breakfast that he was uncomfortable. Most of the stollen Mother had bought from Casey was left over, and she had to make it into bread pudding, which nobody cared for. The next week she took a chance and didn't buy any coffee cake from Casey. Father hauled home three of them and a bag of custard puffs and didn't say a word about her paying for them.

It was a clear victory for Mother, and she kept her advantage. However, it did leave her in the lurch with Casey. She wanted to keep on helping him, for she had somehow got the idea in her head that he needed her business. "I think he works on commission," she said. If so, he couldn't have been banking more than a nickel a week out of us, but she felt it would give him a black eye with his firm if she quit him. She visualized a beetle-browed board of directors meeting every week to scowl at Casey's sales record, so she settled down to buying a weekly loaf of Boston brown bread, a kind of dryish plum pudding. This was the bakery situation at the time my father got the guinea pigs.

If I had been consulted, I would have chosen white mice. You could carry them in your pocket, I had heard, and they would walk up your sleeve and around your shoulders. It was an appealing idea, but about guinea pigs I knew nothing. Neither did Father. He worked for a chemical manufacturer and this put him in touch with medical laboratories, and somebody in one of them asked him if he had any use for some guinea pigs. He accepted four on the spot and brought them home.

"Very unusual colors, too," he told me. "They call them gold and silver." They were tan and gray, and I would have preferred white, but I took them in the spirit they were offered, and Father helped me build cages for them in the basement.

As a means of keeping a boy busy there was something to be said for the guinea pigs. They were hearty eaters and their cages took daily cleaning. Father had designed the cages and he had no use for flimsy construction. The things could have housed small gorillas and to clean them I had to dump them in the back yard, scrub them out, and lug them back to the basement. I had been planning to send off to a mail-order house for a set of muscle builders, $6.95, but taking care of the guinea pigs saved the expense. I sent off for a telescope instead and found it fascinating to inspect the moon with or to inspect the neighborhood in daytime.

By comparison, the guinea pigs were hopeless. They didn't fit my pockets and they had no more personality than a biscuit. Their chief distinction was that they had no tails, and even this palled when I happened to recall that I had no tail either, and that a tail was rather interesting. I wondered if my father would take it unkindly should I try to trade them off to one of my friends, and I felt a few of them out on the subject. None wanted the guinea pigs even as a gift. I had made the mistake of already speaking my mind about them.

As a last resort I might have bred them just for pastime, though God knows what I would have done with still more of the little wretches, but even this was impossible. They were all girl guinea pigs, I found, so I was saddled with a harem. But at this juncture my mother's feeble sales resistance to deliverymen produced a crisis.

She had now been buying Boston brown bread from Casey at the rate of one a week for about two months, and it was stacking up because none of us really cared for it. Although it was still appearing on the table at every meal like a fire horse at the sound of the bell, she had to eat most of it herself and she was getting terribly behind. She took to calling it health bread, but the rest of us felt well enough without it, if not better.

"Just tell the fellow to stop bringing it," Father said. "You've got enough on hand now to feed the starving Armenians." She had four loaves backed up in the breadbox, not counting one she was currently eating her way through. She shook her head vaguely. Father could never understand her feeling about deliverymen even when she pointed out that he worked in a comfortable office while they had to be out in all kinds of weather.

When, finally, she despaired of ever catching up and began to brood over the waste, the guinea pigs at long last came to be a sort of asset. "Do you suppose," she murmured one

day after counting her loaves, "that those animals would eat some of this? Just the stale loaves, of course."

The guinea pigs were vegetarians, but their digestive systems resembled ours. We tried the oldest loaf on them after I chopped it up with my Boy Scout ax, and they went through it in a businesslike way. Mother watched, biting her lip. "At least this isn't wasting it," she said, "and it's very good for them, no doubt."

With this setup going, she grew almost cheerful about the weekly brown-bread purchase and the great help it was being to Casey. However, it began to dawn on me that I was worse off. Now that the guinea pigs were of some use, Mother expected me to keep them indefinitely. I would doubtless have tended them on through their dotage if it had not been for Casey himself.

One day he showed up bearing the brown bread as usual but seeming subtly changed, more assertive. Ordinarily he was an underdog type, which helped Mother feel sorry for him. "This," he announced, "is my last day on the route. You'll have a new man next week."

"You're—quitting?" Mother cried. She really thought he had been fired by the tigerish board of directors she had dreamed up, and she swelled with sympathy and indignation.

"Oh, no—I've been promoted," said Casey. "I'm the new district manager," he told her proudly.

She mechanically took the loaf of Boston brown bread, and it was the last she ever purchased. Her reasoning was obscure but she seemed miffed at the bakery board of directors for deceiving her, as she saw it. She refused to have anything to do with the new man on the route, though she didn't trust herself to face him.

When delivery time approached, the next Friday, she kept a sharp eye out for the bakery truck, borrowing my tele-

scope so she could spot it a couple of blocks away. Then she
closed the front and back doors and hid upstairs until the
new man had come and left, frustrated. After three or four
attempts he gave it up as a bad job, and Mother was free.

Her liberation was followed by mine. As soon as our in-
ventory of brown bread ran out, I hastily swapped the guinea
pigs to a boy who had just moved into the neighborhood
and didn't know about them. He traded me a rubber-band
airplane, and also a good-luck pocket piece which obviously
wasn't doing him a bit of good.

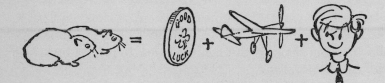

5

THE VINTAGE ALLIGATOR

HE BUILDER WHO HAD CONSTRUCTED OUR HOME in University City was a man who thought big. Extra refinements occurred to him as he went along, and my father had agreed with all of them, not realizing he was running up the cost by three or four thousand dollars. One of the refinements was a wine cellar, a small cavelike nook sealed off from the rest of the basement by a heavy door and bristling with shelves. Mother stored preserves there and called it the fruit cellar, but Father went on calling it the wine cellar since that was what he had been charged for. The only drink he stored there was Bevo, a near-beer made in St. Louis during Prohibition, and it fretted him that he was wasting the wine cellar.

One day he brought home a lug of strange-looking grapes, small and pale. "Concords make a richer-looking jelly," Mother remarked, "but I suppose you got these at a bargain?" He smiled and made another trip from the car carrying a couple of heavy crocks and some rubber tubing. While she peered at this he made a third trip with a box of corks, bottles, and odds and ends.

"I'm going to make wine," he said, in the tone Newton might have used to announce gravitation. "Doc Standish gave me the directions." I was immediately interested. Dr. Standish was a chemist at the company where Father worked, and I had lately been studying fermentation in a physics course at high school. I didn't see how my father could miss with a chemist and me both helping him.

Mother narrowed her eyes. "He's that bachelor, isn't he?"

My father nodded. "He and his mother rent a house in Kirkwood. She's sickly so he doesn't feel right to get married."

Mother sniffed. "I hate to see good grapes wasted. Maybe you ought to talk to Dave before you start." Uncle Dave didn't make wine but he turned out a powerful beer in fortnightly batches. It was muddy at the bottom, and six bottles could have made a horse drunk. Father had no use for it.

"Dave wouldn't be any help," he said shortly. "He's a home-brew man. Wine takes chemistry."

He set up his winery right in the fruit cellar and declined my offer of technical assistance. He was rather secretive about the whole thing since he suspected he was breaking the law and wasn't at all pleased when Mother told him Dave had dropped by to borrow a pipe wrench one afternoon and had inspected the project. By then it was smelling up the basement, and Dave had given the crocks a professional stir with his finger. "Stuff's ripe as limburger," he told Mother. "Ed better watch out or he'll blow up the neighborhood when he bottles it."

"Stuck his *finger* in it?" Father cried when he heard of this. "Dammit, I told you he doesn't know anything about chemistry." He continued to complain about Dave's finger as the wine making went along, but when he took a sample to Dr. Standish, disguised as a bottle of bay rum, he calmed down. The chemist declared it had a nice bouquet and satisfactory authority, and said Father was a fast study. "Serve it with fish and fowl," he said. "Now you need a dessert wine. I'm making a test run of one and I'll give you the formula when I perfect it."

Father felt qualified to start his own test run but he smothered his impatience. Home wine makers were closemouthed, especially Dr. Standish. His elderly mother was a dry and had no idea he was making wine in their basement. She thought he was fiddling around his home laboratory down there, and since she had trouble with stairs he was safe. He also had to drink his wine in the basement or disguise it as a blood tonic upstairs.

When he had the formula set, he passed it along to Father. He called the wine a cream sherry, and Father examined the formula critically when he got it home. "Not enough sugar," he said. "Wine'll be tawny." He made a marginal correction, and Mother frowned.

"You be careful, Ed," she said. "He's a chemist and he ought to know. You'll be blowing up the neighborhood just as Dave said." Father paid no heed.

"I think I ought to help this time," I said. "I'd like to practice my physics."

"This takes experience," he said, making some more changes in the formula. I saw that he had closed the wine-cellar door on me, and I felt slighted. I was sure I could bring some original thinking to the job.

As he got under way with the batch, Dr. Standish suddenly came down on him for a favor he could not refuse, considering everything. "Doc's in a fix," he told Mother. "His mother's arthritis just took a turn for the worse and they have to move to an apartment. He won't have any place to keep his wine."

"Then he'd better drink it," Mother said.

"No time. The office is sending him on an emergency trip to our Miami branch."

"Miami," Mother said. "That's a bachelor for you. They never send you on lovely trips I'd enjoy."

Father started unloading the back seat of his car. It was full of wine bottles wrapped in newspapers, packed in several grocery boxes concealed with a blanket. "What's that?" Mother exclaimed.

"Doc's cream sherry. I promised I'd keep it for him a while." Mother planted her hands on her hips. "Lots of room in the wine cellar," Father said hurriedly, yanking out boxes. "I'll build you shelves somewhere else for your preserves."

Since the smell in the wine cellar was making her giddy every time she went for a glass of jelly, Mother didn't mind being moved out even though she objected on principle. "I hope he has enough manners to send you a crate of oranges from Miami," she said, "but from a bachelor you can't expect anything."

Nevertheless, a token of Dr. Standish's appreciation did arrive from Florida shortly after, but it was not a crate of oranges. It was a sort of pet. I was the one who usually suffered pet trouble in our family, and though it was my father this time, I swiftly became involved because of a chemical experiment I was conducting.

Denied a part in the wine making, I had turned to another product of fermentation—root beer. My grandmother had just made a batch, which gave me the idea. I wrote down her recipe as well as she remembered it, and used our old wash boiler to mix things in, working in our basement where I wouldn't be disturbed. At the last minute I added a touch all my own. I borrowed a bottle of the Standish cream sherry from the wine cellar, and in the interest of science decanted it into the wash boiler. This was the moment my little brother Ted took it into his head to stroll through the basement, so I instantly included him as a silent partner. Together we bottled and corked the roor beer in about thirty assorted bottles I had accumulated, and stashed them in half a dozen spots about the basement in boxes, where they could age and not attract Father's attention. I planned to surprise him with a bottle at dinner soon.

They had been aging for about a week when Dr. Standish's token of appreciation arrived. The box it came in was too small for oranges, and after one look Mother flew inside and left it on the front porch for Father to tackle.

He opened it when he got home. The gift was a Florida alligator, small but genuine. "Kind of a . . . novelty, isn't it?" he said after he had thought about it for a few moments.

"Oh, yes," said Mother, keeping her distance. "I'm pretty sure nobody else in the neighborhood keeps alligators." Father and the alligator looked at each other. "I don't want that thing in the house, Ed," Mother said. "If I were you—"

"I'll build him a pool," he said, brightening up. "Been thinking of building one ever since I saw the one in Mitchell's yard."

"As I was saying," Mother said, "if I were you I'd pick up the phone right now and call the zoo in Forest Park—"

"Oh, I can't do that. It might hurt Doc's feelings." He gathered up the box. "Don't worry—I'll keep him safe in the wine cellar till I build the pool."

He carried the box to the basement, trailed by Ted and me, and he and the alligator advanced into the crowded wine cellar. There he accidentally tipped the box over, and the alligator scuttled for a dark corner. "Get something bigger to put it in," he shouted at me, heading it off with one foot. "Something watertight. Do you know where the wash boiler is?"

I knew quite well where it was. It still smelled root-beery, and I paused to slosh a little water around it while Father shuffled about the wine cellar crying at me to hurry up. He grabbed the alligator by its tail and plopped it into the boiler, breathing hard. "I think they bite," he said. "You boys be careful." He told me to get a rock for an island, and then poured a bucket of water into the boiler. The alligator swam mightily, using both feet and tail, and Ted asked what he was going to name it.

"Alley," said Father, who didn't believe in wasting time.

"Catch some grasshoppers," he said to me. "We'll try him on different things."

The alligator was far more intent on escaping than on eating, though, and the sound of his clawing around the sides of the wash boiler gave my mother gooseflesh every time she went to the basement the following week. Her nerves were already in a state when my root beer took charge. A bottle— one of a group hidden near the water heater—blew up one afternoon. Mother locked the basement door and warned Ted and me, when we got home from school, not to go down there. "Let your father handle this," she cried. "It's his alligator." It was her idea that Alley had got out of his boiler and somehow knocked over a bottle of wine. "I heard it blow up," she declared, "just as Dave said."

When he got home, Father rushed down to see, but found nothing amiss in the wine cellar though he thought the basement smelled more yeasty than usual. "It was all in your mind," he told Mother.

She was getting dinner on the table and had no time to stop and argue, but soon after we sat down, a kind of soft bullet hit the floor from underneath and there was a "Whoomph!"

Mother laid down her fork. "I suppose *that* was all in my mind?" Father rose, frowning. "It's that Standish stuff," she said. "I knew there was something funny about his asking you to keep it."

"Stay here," he said to everybody, and went to the basement. "Nothing wrong in the wine cellar," he reported on his return. "Maybe it's the sewer line. Have you been running coffee grounds down the sink again?"

"I certainly have n—" Mother began as he sat down, when there came another "Whoomph" from the depths. Father rose as if kicked, and this time we all streaked down to the basement after him.

"Be careful, Ed!" Mother cried as he yanked open the wine

cellar door. "Watch out for the alligator!" she screeched into his ear.

He swung the door wide. "See for yourself. The wine's all right."

Mother peered in. "Which is that Standish stuff? Is it all there? Did you count?"

In a tone of extreme patience he began to count off the Standish bottles out loud. I wondered if anyone would mind if I went back and finished my dinner. "By George!" Father said, rather blankly. He counted again. "There was an even two dozen. Now there's only twenty-three."

"See?" Mother said. "The stuff's going off."

He shook his head in a baffled way. "But there have been *three* explosions—"

Suddenly there was another "Whoomph" elsewhere in the basement. Father jumped backwards out of the wine cellar. "Where was that one?" he yelled. It was under the stairs where six bottles were aging, but only Ted and I knew it. Father lifted his nose. "Something down here smells funny," he said, and looked at me.

I cleared my throat. "Well, I've got a little root beer—" I said, and was interrupted by another "Whoomph" from under the stairs. This time my father tracked it. He dashed over and jerked off a sack with which I had concealed this batch. He nudged the box out with his foot while the two blown bottles geysered over the others.

"Stand back!" he cried. "Another might go any second."

Another did just then, but from somewhere else in the basement, and Father leaped back, shielding his face. "Where was that one?" he shouted, looking wildly about as if surrounded by snipers.

"It may be over by the water heater," I said.

"*May* be?" He stared at me. "How many places have you got this dynamite?"

Ted spoke up before I could. "Five!" he said. "We got lots more bottles."

Mother spun him around. "Upstairs," she said in a command tone. "Everybody. I'm not going to have my good meal get cold over a lot of foolishness." We all returned upstairs and sat down at the table again, Father rather heavily. There was tension in the air, accented from time to time by the root beer below.

"Now," Father said when we had finished eating, "I want to know what this is all about."

"It was an experiment," I said. "You wouldn't let me help with the wine, and Grandmother had a recipe for root—"

"I might have known," he said. "Your grandmother again." Mother gave him a look and he looked right back. "And you," he said to her, "have the nerve to complain about my wine."

"We got wine in ours too," Ted piped up proudly. I could have killed him. My father paled.

"Wine!" he said. "So that's where that bottle of Doc's wine went!" He started to his feet.

"Just a minute, Ed," Mother said. "You see? There wasn't a thing wrong with Mom's root beer recipe. It was that wine that made it blow up." She looked pleased. "You even said yourself the wine formula was all wrong."

He gritted his teeth. "Dammit, that's not the point. I gave my word I'd take good care of his wine, and now look what's happened—!"

"I suppose it's all right if we get bombed, just so you keep your word," she said. Another bottle of root beer, from a batch directly under the dining room, blew up at that moment and we all jumped.

Perhaps realizing the issue was getting as muddy as Dave's beer, Father abandoned it. "Don't you go near that wine cellar again, young man," he said, wheeling toward me. "Understand?" He started to stalk out, and then a bit of poetic justice occurred to him and he turned back. "You can start tomorrow digging the pool in the back yard for the alligator," he said. "Do something constructive for a change. I'll show you where I want it."

He picked a spot near the rear. There in the twilight he drew with a stick the outline of his pool. I was too shocked to speak for a moment. I was expecting something no bigger than a bathtub, but the hole he envisioned could swallow up a small automobile. It was at least half again as large as the only other neighborhood pool, and I thought it best to point this out while there was still time. He nodded. "Yes—old man Mitchell's. I had that in mind."

He told me to make it four feet deep in the middle and two at the sides, and I began digging the next afternoon. It did keep me out of the explosive basement, though the root beer had slowed down after twelve or fifteen blasts. I had lost my taste for it anyway. It smelled pretty punk.

As the week wore on, Mother gradually grew restive about my tracking mud into the house from the digging, and when I went at it for the fourth day she called a halt. "Go get that alligator," she said. "It's all right for you to go to the wine cellar just for that." I got him.

"Now dump him," she said, getting out of the way. I dumped the wash boiler, and Alley headed for the nearest shrubbery. "I'll handle your father," she said. "I've had enough alligator."

"Anyway, he can always put goldfish in the pool, like Mr. Mitchell," I said.

"Hm-m," she said. "So he can. You'd better fill that hole up." I looked at her in surprise. "I've seen that Mitchell pool," she said. "They get full of guck."

I started to shovel earth back into the hole. "Wait," she cried. "Get the root beer." I brought it from the basement, handling it tenderly. "Throw it in," she said. "We'll kill two birds with one stone." I stood well back of the earth fort I had dug out, and tossed it in, one bottle at a time, and the effect was remarkable. As root beer it was a failure, but if I had been trying for TNT I might have had something. Then I hurried to fill the fizzy hole before Father got home.

Mother met him in the yard as he stood staring at where his pool had lately been growing. "I had to do something with that root beer," she said crisply. "With that dangerous wine in it—"

"You didn't touch the rest of Doc's wine?" Father cried. He turned putty-colored, and she let him hang for a few seconds.

"No," she said, and while he was weak with relief she told him she had turned the alligator loose since there wasn't going to be any pool for him, and he could tell Dr. Standish it was all her fault. He took the news almost calmly. He had been getting tired of sharing the wine cellar with Alley, and now he was free to give his whole attention to his cream sherry, which was threatening to get out of its crock.

The only report we ever received on Alley was roundabout. Mr. Mitchell found his goldfish were mysteriously disappearing that summer. He told my father he thought cats must be getting them, and Father said he wouldn't be surprised. Mr. Mitchell bought an air rifle to defend himself and turned out to be a fair shot up to thirty feet, though his smaller goldfish kept right on disappearing. It was a hard summer on cats in the neighborhood, but apparently a splendid one for alligators.

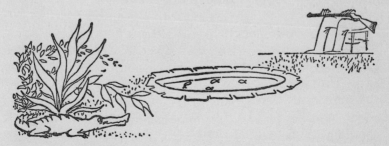

6

OSCAR, THE CAMPUS DOG

OWNED A SHORT AND RATHER LONGISH DOG named Faegae (usually pronounced to rhyme with ouija) at the time I left home to attend the University of Missouri. Faegae was a cur, but I thought of him as a successful hybrid. He was a happy dog and a brainy one, and it was harder for me to leave him behind than it was to leave my parents and Ted, who could get along quietly without me.

My uneasiness over Faegae turned out to be tragically well founded. I had not been gone two months when word came that my dog had been hit by a truck near Delmar Boulevard and done in. I had never let him go so far from home alone. He had, I suspected, been searching for me at the time, and if I had not been up to my ears in studying and in pledge duties at my fraternity house, I would have felt my loss more keenly.

Still, I felt bad enough, and it led me into an association that for sheer social awkwardness was in a class by itself. I took up with Oscar, the campus dog, and it was almost as bad as if I had become buddy-buddy with the village drunkard.

Oscar was a blowsy Airedale belonging to no one. He cadged food where he could and slept where he pleased. He was popular with the male students and with outdoorsy types of girls. But he made few advances and was, in fact, rather gruff, which was why most of the coeds eyed him with alarm.

I knew him in only a casual way until the day I learned of my own dog's passing. That afternoon, on my way home from a late class, I ran across Oscar sauntering along the red campus in his go-to-hell fashion, and I stopped to scratch him. He got a good deal of patting but not much scratching, and I knew all the good places. He changed course and followed me as far as my fraternity house, where I bade him good-by for the present. He did not try to follow me in. We were located in a shabby old place on Hitt Street, but I don't think Oscar was being a snob. Apparently he had other business to take care of and had escorted me home only out of gratitude for the scratching. Since I was merely a pledge, I felt it just as well not to risk irritating any paddle-happy actives by bringing a dog in.

Actually, though, Oscar had followed me home in order to fix my dwelling in his mind, I discovered. He liked to know where to locate students with special abilities. I found this out the following Saturday evening when he paid me a call.

I was alone in my room, a back one on the second floor, studying. Both my roommates were out on dates, as were most of the other members who were not pledges such as I and thereby more restricted. On the first floor the lights were dimmed, Rudy Vallee was twanging from the record player, and each of four strategically separated sofas in the big living room cuddled an active and his date. It was a cheap and popular way to spend a quiet Saturday evening. The housemother left open the door to her room but she stayed in it and it was off to itself, opening on the dining hall, which adjoined the living room.

Rudy was just sailing into a whimsy about love when Oscar stalked up the front porch steps and into the foyer, where he paused to adjust his eyes to the faint light. There were startled mutters from two of the actives who could just barely make him out from their sofas at the front end of the room. He turned their way and in a businesslike manner made the rounds of all the sofas, sniffing for me.

The girls, none of whom were among Oscar's intimates, shrieked and leaped. Oscar hurriedly trotted on through to the dining hall and paused at the doorway to the house-mother's room. She was Mrs. Abernathy, a critical old biddy whom we pledges had to entertain by turns, listening to rec-ollections of her better times at fraternities more socially prominent than ours. Mrs. Abernathy was just hustling out to investigate the riot in the living room, and she and Oscar met at her doorway. As a matter of fact she tripped over him and nearly fell flat. She howled and caught herself on one of the dining tables. Oscar dashed out the dining-hall entry to the foyer, growling. Untangling himself from the legs of the dating couples, who were bolting out for quieter parts, he headed groggily up the front stairway and smelled his way down the hall to my room.

I was wondering about the noise downstairs, and when Os-car arrived I put two and two together. Mrs. Abernathy was tearing off screeches in between Rudy's croons, and I hurried down after shutting Oscar in my room.

The housemother was the only living soul on the first floor when I got there, though she was noisy enough for a dozen. There had been little light for her to see Oscar by, and she had made up her mind she had fallen over a prowler casing the joint on hands and knees. She hurried about, switching on every light, and would have locked the front door if it had not been against house rules. I tried to soothe her and started back upstairs to get rid of Oscar, but Mrs. Abernathy grabbed me.

"You stay down here with me," she cried. "That thug may come back!"

I told her I could almost guarantee that he wouldn't, but

it had no effect. She was hysterical, I decided, and might even follow me upstairs, an unthinkable breach of house etiquette. I would have called one of my fellow pledges to help, but they were in a bull session on the third floor and hadn't noticed anything unusual.

There was nothing to do but keep Mrs. Abernathy company until the actives began getting home from their dates. I persuaded her to return to her room, where she brewed us a pot of tea to settle our stomachs.

Luckily, the first man home was not one of the group scattered by Oscar. I left him listening goggle-eyed to Mrs. Abernathy's tale of a muscular rapist traveling on all fours through the dining hall, and sneaked back upstairs. I woke up Oscar, hauled him down the back stairs to the kitchen and outside, and got back a few seconds before Bruce Endler came charging in. Bruce, a junior in business administration, was one of those whom Oscar had surprised in the living room and he had an idea I had somehow arranged it, for I had been seen hobnobbing with the dog. I told Bruce I had been busy with my studies all evening until some kind of rowdyism had broken out downstairs, and he gave me five licks with his paddle for being fresh. The three other actives who had been run out of their sofas later kept me up for an hour, questioning me between paddlings because my room smelled doggy to them.

Though my name was linked with Oscar's, they couldn't prove anything as long as I declined to testify against myself, but they brought it up at chapter meeting Monday evening. Being a pledge, I didn't attend meetings, but I was cited for suspicion and there were hints that I would cease to be even a pledge if anything else happened around there involving Oscar.

I feared the dog was going to ruin me, and I took to avoiding him. This was difficult, but a ray of hope suddenly showed up soon after. The house we occupied was, as I said, shabby. Midway through the semester our commissary officer, who handled all financial matters, made a deal for a new place. It was a handsome southern colonial mansion on Richmond Avenue. We arranged to move between semesters, and all the boys were greatly cheered because it was so fine a house and was happily surrounded by sororities, too. I was glad for an additional reason. The place was a good six blocks from our old one and not on Oscar's regular beat.

By the time we moved in I had been initiated as an active member of the fraternity. A dramatic feature of the initiation was the burning of a brand on one's left chest with a red-hot iron. I hardly felt a thing, I was so relieved to be achieving a status Oscar could no longer place in total jeopardy, but I didn't realize how much damage he could still do, given the proper stage setting.

Now that we had an adequate house the membership voted to hold our formal spring dance there instead of at the Daniel Boone Hotel. This particular dance was a big one on our social calendar, and we wanted to show the place off. In the rear garden of our new mansion there was a terrace with a summerhouse at one end, and to give a garden-party feel, one of the boys who was taking engineering volunteered to build a small lagoon there. He was Paul Pratt, a bashful lad who didn't seem to care for girls. It gave him a lot of spare time and he was a bear for work. He started right off and as his enthusiasm grew he added a broad flagstone walk encircling the lagoon, stone benches, and a little fountain.

I joined his work party for a time but had to desert on the week end before the dance. I had decided it was time I had my own dinner jacket, or tuxedo as we called them, instead of renting one. I got a ride to St. Louis in one of the boys' Model A's, feeling that my father might be so glad to see me, he would let me buy the tux on his account at Famous-Barr. It worked, and the trip was marred by only one thing. As we

pulled out from the curb in front of the fraternity house, I
saw Oscar, who hadn't figured out yet where I had moved
to, trotting down Richmond toward us. I was sitting in the
rumble seat, as exposed as a fireplug. His ears pricked up and
he uttered a surprised little bark. Stretching his neck, he set
out after the car at a rolling gait he had.

"Hurry up," I yelled through the back window. "Here
comes Oscar."

We whipped around the corner and roared on past the
baseball diamond and the field house, pursued by the dog.
After a couple of blocks he gave up and watched us zoom
off. Then he turned and trotted back the way he had come,
and I had a sinking feeling he knew all.

When we returned from the trip Sunday evening, Oscar
was hanging around the sidewalk in front of the new house.
As I climbed out of the rumble seat, he rushed up and pawed

me cordially. "Take my suit in with you," I said from the side
of my mouth to one of the boys. I scratched Oscar's chest
and strolled away as if I lived somewhere down the street. He
followed five paces behind, looking skeptical, and when his
attention was diverted by an uproar from a sorority house
across the street, I skipped through a hedge and made my
way back across other sorority-house lawns, at some risk of
being taken for a peeping Tom.

Oscar was checked for the time being but not discouraged.
He included our new neighborhood in his rounds, offending
the sororities there, and I had to memorize all the nearby
trees and shrubbery suitable for hiding behind if I saw him
first.

The lagoon project was completed almost on the eve of the
dance, looking very festive, and our bashful engineer was
flustered by the praise, especially from some of the seniors.
They were quite taken by a dramatic touch Paul had given
his lagoon with a couple of floodlights at each side of the
glass doors that opened onto the terrace. At their urging he
located the lights at floor level though he thought this was too
low. He underestimated the boys. On the night of the dance
when couples began strolling out to the terrace, the filmy
skirts of the girls passed in front of the floodlights and it was
as revealing as a burlesque show. More interesting, too, since
we knew most of the cast personally. But for the time being
most of us, and especially Paul, didn't realize what was in
store.

I had no time to speculate on it anyway. At the last minute my date for the dance sprained her ankle in the bathtub.
She was terribly upset and wanted to substitute one of her
sorority sisters for me, but I said no, thanks. Every sorority
had one or two sisters who couldn't have got a date without
offering a cash bonus. Instead, I hastily buttonholed one of

my fraternity brothers from Texas. Texans, for some rare reason, always had nice spare girls on tap.

"Why sure," this one said, "this little Houston gal, this Ellen Sue. 'Course she had her a date, boy, she's that cute. But the varmint got called out of town so that's how come. Pretty as a bug."

I didn't care about the rest of it as long as Ellen Sue was attractive and free. He phoned her the good news and said I'd call for her at nine o'clock.

As it happened, I was delayed. Now that I had my own tuxedo I scorned to wear a ready-made bow tie, but when I started to tie the one I had bought, it stopped me cold. After fighting with me for ten or fifteen minutes it ended up in a drunken slant, looking bushed, and my arms were so tired I could hardly hold them up. Happily, there was one lad in the house who knew the trick, and I hurried to his room.

I found him already doing this service for another brother, and a waiting line of eight, all wearing ties as tipsy as mine, stretched into the hallway. I got in line. Already it was past nine, and our expert worked slowly. He had to place his subject in front of a mirror and then work from behind as if tying the bow on himself. I timed him at three minutes each, and when I finally got waited on I was getting close to being an hour late for my Texas date.

I set out for her sorority house some five blocks away at a sprint. In my haste I forgot all about Oscar, whom I had grown used to looking for sharply first. He was on the sidewalk but for a wonder he was looking the other way, and I had time to jump through a gap in a hedge and detour him. I could hear him sniffing the air as I sped off across lawns and when I arrived at the sorority house I was blowing and feeling a little damp from perspiration and from the hedge, which had been wet. I apologized to Ellen Sue for being late, but didn't feel I cared to explain about my tie, though she waited.

"Well," she said, tapping her little foot, "seeing's you're here, let's do be getting on, if the band's still playing." She was quite pretty, a blue-eyed Texas blonde. She was not tall but she was wearing three-inch heels and looked as if she would be a good dancer.

I offered her my arm and led her outside. "This way," I said when she paused on the sidewalk, staring around. "Our house is on Richmond, you know." She did not answer, and I hurried her along, trying to take short steps for her convenience while she hung like a sack on my right arm. For two blocks I did all the talking, which seemed odd to me because all the other Texas girls I knew would talk your ears off. I had about decided she was an exotic quiet type when she gave me a clue to her silence.

"I—do—declare," she snapped between gasps, "th' taxis— are doin'—mighty poorly this evenin'!"

For some reason, perhaps my anxiety over being delayed, it had not occurred to me to call a cab. I seldom needed one for myself, but it was the usual way to call for a girl encumbered with a long formal gown. I flushed in the darkness and mumbled something about having been in a hurry. She did not reply but got a firmer grip on my arm, and I dragged her along for another couple of blocks.

We turned the corner into Richmond Avenue and were within sight of the house when I suddenly remembered about Oscar. I slowed down to peer around. It was not a well-lighted street. Ellen Sue's fingernails dug into my biceps and she darted little glances about. "Whatever's the matter?" she chirped.

"Sh-h-h," I said hastily. "He might still be hanging around."

She shoved her evening purse into my coat pocket and gripped my arm with both her hands. Like most of the Texas girls I knew, she was surprisingly strong, as if she did weight-lifting on the side.

"Here he comes right now!" I whispered. Though she did not notice him, I had spotted Oscar. He was crossing Richmond diagonally toward us, about a hundred feet away. "Quick," I said, and whisked my date through the handy gap in the hedge I had used earlier that evening. I was thinking of her as much as of myself, remembering Oscar's bad habit of jumping up and pawing. Ellen Sue failed to appreciate my thoughtfulness. Shrieking slightly, she shook her full skirt loose from the damp hedge.

"Here comes *who*, for mercy sakes?" she cried, in a voice anyone on the street could hear.

I hastily hauled her along the lawn behind the hedge, toward my fraternity's front lawn. "Oscar!" I hissed into her ear. "And do be quiet unless you want to get mauled."

She gave me a shocked look and abruptly let go of me. This helped, and I was able to boost her over our own hedge, a low privet, by picking her up under the arms, and then drag her into the house before Oscar could pick up our trail. She dashed for the powder room, breathing hard, and stayed there twenty minutes. I had begun to wonder if she had fainted or was taking a bath, when she reappeared, frosty but poised, and I led her onto the dance floor.

As I had suspected, Ellen Sue was a good dancer, expert at the peculiar style then rampant at the University of Missouri, in which the girl leaned forward from the waist in an inverted letter L and kept her feet out of your way. The stag line spotted her technique at once and began cutting in. She seemed relieved by it though I was beginning to enjoy myself for the first time that evening. I sauntered out to the newly appointed terrace, ignoring signals from brothers who were stuck with girls nobody wanted to cut in on, and had a look around.

The little lagoon fountain was sparkling in the strong

beams of the low-placed floodlights, and there were pleasant murmurings from couples in the summerhouse a little distance off. The author of this setting, Paul the bashful engineer, was out there too, probably avoiding the dance floor, and I complimented him.

As we stood there, intermission time arrived. Couples began streaming out the doorway, and for the first time it struck me how cunningly the floodlights were placed. "Hey," I said to Paul in an undertone as the girls' pretty legs passed in review. "Will you look at that!" The only sound from the young engineer was a sort of strangling one, and I wrenched my gaze from the legs to him. His face had turned purplish. He spoke between clenched teeth:

"By hell," he muttered, "so this is why they wanted the cruddy lights so low!" From him this was strong language.

"Now, now—take it easy, Paul," I said as he moved forward, arms swinging from his shoulders. "No harm done." He shook me off.

"One of these girls could be your sister or mine!" he snapped, bursting away. I didn't know what he had in mind to do, but something happened just then that took all my attention.

Inside the house there were sudden girlish shrieks verging on panic, and then I heard my name being roared by some of my fraternity brothers. I had been about to go inside and hunt up Ellen Sue to claim her for the intermission, but I was saved the trouble. She burst out of the doorway at that instant through the floodlight beams, and the cause of her speed was Oscar. He was right behind her, not chasing her as she probably thought, but looking for me. I grabbed the scruff of his neck, for he disdained collars. "I'll be right back, Ellen Sue," I said, yanking Oscar toward the steps.

She clutched her skirt clear of me, and I noticed it had been clawed—by Oscar, I had no doubt, as were some other skirts here and there. "Don't you bother your haid!" she said hotly in Texas accents.

"But Oscar isn't my dog, Ellen Sue—" I started to protest, but at that moment the floodlights went out, killed at the switch by our betrayed engineer. In the confusion that followed, argument was useless. Besides, Ellen Sue darted away, and Oscar was trying to get loose. I gathered him to my chest against my stiff shirt front and carried him struggling into the house.

If I dumped him outside, I knew he would come right back, so I carried him up to my room, alarming couples who were settling down for intermission on the lower flight of the stairway. My room in the new house was on the third floor, shared with a devil-may-care lad named Jones, and I didn't think he'd mind. I closed our door on Oscar, quite sure he would be imprisoned for the rest of the evening.

He was, indeed. He had a much better evening than I did, for Ellen Sue could hardly bring herself to speak civilly to me again when she had to ask me for her purse, which was squashed in my pocket, and she refused to let me take her out for a bite to eat after the dance.

I took her home, in a cab this time, feeling she would have preferred I sit in front with the driver, and she declined coldly when I offered to have her skirt mended. It was a flimsy thing anyway, I thought, as the floodlight had plainly shown.

I returned home in my mussed tuxedo sprinkled with Oscar's hair, and when I arrived he was waiting with a last surprise. Jonesey was already back. I hadn't had a chance to tell him Oscar was a temporary resident in our room, so it had been a shock when he walked in. Now he pointed to the floor, not yet trusting himself to speak. The carpet was littered with bits of paper, in the midst of which Oscar was lying, chewing with difficulty.

"You know what this damn dog of yours did?" Jones yelled. "He found that box my mother sent me and ate it all up, every last damn thing!"

So he had—a marble cake, a hunk of salami, salted nuts, and some soft cheese and crackers. He had even gone through a box of taffy and was now finishing it, stuck to his teeth.

Jones had counted on the box to see him through the next week for late snacks. He was studying advertising and it made him ravenous. To make it up to him I had to buy him goodies for that period from the sandwich man who made the rounds of the houses late every evening. It cost me $2.80, and I took what comfort I could in the fact the stolen feast upset Oscar's stomach. Although I was severely criticized at the next chapter meeting for inciting riot at the dance, Oscar avoided me for a good while afterwards almost as vigorously as did Ellen Sue, and on the whole I felt safer without either of them.

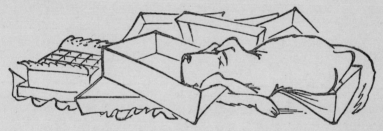

7

THE HONEYMOON HOUND

A DOG WAS THE LAST THING I WANTED TO TAKE along on a honeymoon. My bride felt the same way about it, but we were puppets of fate. Both of us had a weakness for animals, and in fact it had a good deal to do with our getting married.

When I met her I didn't know she adored animals. I was working for a small weekly newspaper—called the *Suburban Watchdog,* by happy chance—and she was employed in the same building and in a nearby office. We met at the water cooler in the hall, and even in the dim light there I was stunned by her lovely Irish eyes and pert nose. She forgave me for drenching her with ice water when my hand shook, and I saw she was a jewel. There was no time to lose, for I had an offer to work for the *St. Louis Globe-Democrat* and I was leaving the *Watchdog* shortly. I loaned her my handkerchief to mop herself off with, found her name was Pat, and asked if I could phone her at home sometime after she dried out.

A reporter's hours on the *Globe,* a morning paper, made problems for romance because I worked from two in the afternoon till ten or later at night, but one Saturday evening the city editor called me over with a glint in his eye. "I want an early-morning story on the zoo," he said. "Get yourself out there at 6:00 A.M. and see what's doing."

I phoned Pat. "If you're free tomorrow night," I said, "I'd like to see you. I've got an ungodly sunrise assignment, so I'll be off early. Going to the zoo at 6:00 A.M."

"That sounds like fun," she said. "Could I go along?"

She sounded balmy to me, but I took her along and she was a big help. She spotted one of the ostriches laying an egg right out in the open, in its yard, and when I ran myself dizzy finding a keeper to rescue it, this won her devotion. I was merely trying to improve the feature story I wrote, but she took it as a tribute to the mamma ostrich, and we were engaged in no time. I then became acquainted with her pet dog, Socks.

He was a crossbreed, gaunt and surly, with one yellow eye and one brown one, both rather bloodshot. His wiry coat was quilted with cowlicks so that he always looked upset. He disapproved of me, having favored an earlier suitor who worked for a packing company and probably smelled delicious, and I didn't care greatly for him. I certainly didn't plan to take him on our honeymoon. To give her credit, neither did Pat.

We were going to take a little trip through part of the Ozark Mountains of southern Missouri. As I loaded Pat's luggage in my convertible coupe, I suddenly noticed she was holding Socks on a leash as if ready to join the party.

"We're just going to drop him off at Aubuchon's Kennel on the way," she whispered, a finger to her lips.

I opened the door for her, and Socks got in. He planted himself in the middle of the seat and banged his head loudly on an overhead strut. "I guess you'll have to put the top down," Pat murmured.

Fortunately the day was clear, though breezy. We squeezed in on each side of Socks, who had his bony body well braced. I jammed my hat down over my ears and off we went.

With Socks in the middle, conversation was difficult. He snuffled the air, and once when we passed a traffic policeman he nearly blew the man out of his shoes, leaning hard across Pat with a thunderous roar. A block from the kennel he grew tense, and when I parked in front he remained solidly in the seat. We were hauling at his leash when the Mrs. Aubuchon who ran the kennel came running out. "Leave him set," she bawled.

Pat stared at her. "This is Socks," she said. "Remember—? I phoned you—"

"Hound, you said," Mrs. Aubuchon replied coldly. "Little beagle hound, I thought. I got no room for grizzly bears." She hurried back inside.

We got back in the car. "Know of any other kennels around here?" I asked, out loud since Socks was now wise to us.

"Maybe we'll pass one on the way," Pat said, though kennels in the Ozarks were scarcer than teetotalers. Socks was relaxed and happy, all set for a honeymoon. He leaned on me till my right arm went to sleep, and after a stop at a roadside stand for lunch he and Pat changed places. Sitting together we felt more like honeymooners, but the pause for lunch raised the question of feeding Socks. He had had a hamburger with us, without onion. I stopped at a little country store, but the stock was largely plug tobacco and canned goods. I bought a couple of cans of beans on speculation, and the proprietor threw in an old loaf of bread, so stale it could have been a weapon.

"Oh, lovely," Pat said when I returned to the car. "He adores baked beans. Bread, too." She could have gone on for hours. With his frame to support Socks couldn't be choosy. "I guess we'd better push right along now," she said. "I'd like to get to the hotel in time to clean up and stroll around before dinner."

I had made reservations at a resort hotel on the Gasconade River, an attractive place favored by family vacationers and quieter conventions. We felt we would attract less attention there, but we hadn't counted on Socks. We drove into a parking area beside the broad lawn at four o'clock. A few women were playing a sedate form of tennis on some courts adjoining, watched by a gallery of other women.

"Schoolteachers," Pat whispered. She was right, though I didn't know how she knew. The teachers were having a convention there. We got out of the car, and I fetched our luggage while Pat took charge of Socks, who was now quite agreeable to leaving the car.

"Let's try to act as if we've been married for years," she whispered. We headed for the hotel's front entrance. Pat, gripping the leash, smiled sunnily at the teachers as we passed, and I bowed as well as I could with my arms full of suitcases. We needn't have bothered. The teachers hardly noticed us. They were staring at Socks. Looking larger and more tousled than usual after his windy trip, he was making rapidly for the hotel, towing Pat along at a skip. Preparations for dinner were under way, and the air had an enticing pork-roast smell. Pat was sprinting when they reached the doorway and she and Socks shot into it and disappeared while I trundled along behind.

They were already at the room clerk's counter at the other side of the lobby when I entered the doorway, and though the lobby was fairly crowded, mainly with teachers, there was a wide swath where Pat and Socks had just passed. Also quite a bit of excited murmuring.

I lumbered through the swath with my bags, looking pleasantly from side to side. The room clerk, standing well back from his counter but keeping Socks in his line of vision, spoke up while I was still eight or ten feet away. "Sorry, no vacancies," he said, pronouncing it as one word.

I eased the luggage to the floor. "We have reservations," I said. If there were any bellboys they must have seen us coming, for none appeared. I identified myself to the clerk.

"You didn't say anything about a—" He leaned over the counter. "That's a dog, isn't it?"

"Certainly he's a dog," said Pat, who had been quiet till now, struggling to keep Socks from dragging her into the

dining room. "He's my pet dog. He goes everywhere with me. With us I mean."

"This is a nice place," said the room clerk. "No dogs."

"Where's the manager?" I said. "Dammit, I have my reserva—"

"Come on, honey," Pat said abruptly, turning back toward the entrance. "If they're going to act this way, I don't care to stay."

"They can't do—" I said, and found I was talking to air. Pat was on her way to the dining room, skidding backwards on the soles of her shoes, the leash taut as a guy wire behind her.

"Help!" she said. Instantly there was a lively flow of guests to the outdoors. I abandoned the luggage and went to her rescue. I outweighed Socks, though he was in better shape. I wrapped his leash around one wrist and dragged him across the emptied lobby.

"I'll come back for the luggage," I shouted over my shoulder.

"Never mind!" the room clerk bawled. He darted from behind his counter, seized the luggage and trotted it out after us. He dropped the bags beside the car and scurried back inside while we reloaded.

"Don't let it bother you," I said to Pat as we rolled away, followed by acid comments from a swirl of teachers peeking around shrubbery. "We'll find another place easily."

"It was too crowded there anyway," she said. "I felt conspicuous."

We passed several motels in the next half hour but didn't fancy them, though Socks was now giving every place an earnest, hungry scrutiny, and my own stomach felt awfully empty. "You'll eat when we do," Pat said to him, shoving to get a little more room. "Just remember, going along was your own idea."

I slowed down as another motel came in sight. "Looks pretty fair. And it's getting on toward dusk."

"The cottages are attractive," Pat said, "and I guess that's the owner standing out front. He looks like a nice man."

It was the owner. He was smiling a welcome in front of the office, on which was a sign that read VACANCY spelled out in lights. As we turned into the drive, he spied Socks and his smile faded. He jabbed a button and more lights popped on in the sign. It now read NO VACANCY.

"Well, for heaven's sake—" Pat said, but the owner had retreated into his office.

We returned to the open road and drove on. We discovered we were growing much less particular. We were willing to stop anywhere now, but the next two motels had no vacancies, and the third one had none as soon as they noticed Socks.

"One thing in our favor," I said. "The darker it gets, the less of him they can see. By midnight he ought to be invisible."

"Let's stop and put the top up," Pat said. "I don't care if he does bump his head. It'll help hide him."

It turned out to be a brilliant stroke, or so it seemed at the time. Though Socks grumbled at having to ride with his neck bent, he was not observed by the next motel man, especially since I took care to park in a shadowy spot and approach the office on foot. This motel was a rustic sort with small imitation-log cottages scattered widely over three or four acres of wooded hillside. The small office and a good-sized dining room were similar in style. Dinner was being served at the moment, smelling glorious, and a cottage was available.

"I'll show you the way," the proprietor said, but I backed to the door and told him we wouldn't think of troubling him.

He hesitated, then smiled in a fatherly manner. "Of

course," he said. "Just follow the trail and you'll find it all right. Cottage number seven, one of my best."

The trail, carpeted with pine needles and just wide enough for one car, wound up among the trees to our cottage. "That's a lucky number, seven," Pat said. "We're going to like this place."

I said the man seemed very hospitable. I was glad it was one of his best cottages, for even it was none too special. Its door was merely a screen door opening on a tiny porch across the front. A screen-covered window also looked out over the porch, and inside, the cottage was all one room with a corner walled off for a small bathroom and a closet. The bed was an old-fashioned iron one on castors, and we tied Socks to one leg of it with his leash. He had shown so much interest in the aromas from the dining room that we didn't trust the screens to keep him in. Even after he was connected to the bed Pat felt nervous about him.

"You'd better give him one of his cans of beans now," she said. "If he gets to baying, he can wake the dead."

I went after the beans and then remembered something I should have thought of hours before. I had no can opener, and a tire pump and jack seemed a poor substitute. Instead, I brought Socks the stale bread. It felt like hickory, but he drooled at it and went right to work, holding it between his big front paws and trying to bite a chunk off the end.

"I hope it'll last him till we get back," Pat said.

I felt sure it would. He was already trying the other side of his jaws on the hardtack. In his flaming youth he had had distemper, and his back teeth were in bad shape. We latched the screen door on the outside and went hand in hand down the pine-needle trail by flashlight to the dining room.

There, as we started up the steps to the porch, a large black shape suddenly loomed up. Pat squeaked and grabbed my arm as I was trying to aim the flashlight. The shape rose to its hind feet, planted its front ones on my shoulders, and tasted my face.

"Step right in, folks," said the proprietor, appearing in the doorway. He smiled at Pat and opened the screen door. "Down, Homer, sir."

"Wh—who's Homer?" Pat cried.

"My Great Dane, ma'am," he said. "Weighs 160 pounds."

It happened to be what I weighed at the time, though I wore it differently. If the Dane had used a hat, it would have been about size thirty. I lowered him back to the porch floor and discouraged him from following us into the dining room.

"He took a liking to you," the proprietor said, regarding me with interest. "Acted like he smelled dog on you."

"Yes, I pet them," I said quickly.

"*He* knows," said the man, winking. I felt sure he knew too much, and I was glad he couldn't talk.

As we went through a good meal of fried chicken and biscuits, I noticed presently that Pat kept making small biscuit sandwiches of dark meat, which she hid in a paper napkin beside the sugar bowl like a squirrel preparing for winter. "For Socks," she whispered when she noticed me eying her hoard. "I can't very well come right out and ask for some scraps."

"How about Homer? He'll smell it when we walk out of here."

She shook her head. "I'll put it in my bag." I had not yet been married long enough to know that a wife's purse was an answer to almost any small transportation emergency. In this case, though, it wasn't needed. Homer the Dane was not in sight when we left the dining room, and we scurried back up the trail feeling cheerful.

"Wait a minute," Pat said when we reached number seven and I started up the steps to open the screen door. Inside, we could hear old Socks grinding away on his stale bread, stopping to pant hoarsely now and then. "Before I feed him the stuff, he ought to take his evening run."

I gave her the flashlight to aim in the cottage window while I went inside and unleashed Socks from the bed. "But I'll keep the leash on him while we're out," I said.

"Yes," she murmured. "Don't let's take any chances." They were thrust upon us a few seconds later. Just as I got Socks unhitched from the bed leg, separated from his loaf, and had hauled him to the screen door, the flashlight went out. There was a scream in the night, Pat's voice. I heard her scampering up the porch steps as I shoved the screen door open, and we collided.

"Get back inside," she shrieked. "*He's* out here."

The thud of heavy paws followed her up the steps. "Queeick! Close the screen door," she cried.

I tried to, but Socks, snarling in a fierce, slobbery manner, was in the way. I clipped him one with my knee and fumbled blindly for the screen-door handle. I got instead a handful of Great Dane, and Homer took it for a gesture of hospitality. He started in the doorway, and I fell backward over Socks, who was trying to leave between my legs.

"The flashlight!" I roared to Pat. "Turn on the flashlight." But she had dropped the flashlight outside. She raced across my chest to the screen door and yanked it shut. I sat up in the dark, wondering if high heels could mark one for life.

"Have you got Socks?" she said suddenly. I could hear his throaty growl, strangely muffled, but I couldn't see him in the dark. "Good heavens," she said. "I think they're *both* outside."

I started to get up and there was an abrupt scuffling somewhere on the floor. "Oh, my," Pat cried. "I think they're both *inside*."

I remembered noticing a light switch somewhere on the far wall. I went over there on hands and knees and felt my way to it.

Only Socks was in sight inside. He had retrieved his precious loaf and had it crosswise in his jaws. He was glaring out through the window screen, horrible growls filtering through the bread each time he exhaled. Outside we could hear Homer circling the cottage, leaving a trail of snuffles. In her excitement Pat had dropped on the ground the sandwiches she had prepared for Socks. "Now he'll never go away," she lamented, peeking out. "We'll have to keep Socks tied to the bed all night. If that dog comes up on the porch again, Socks will go right through the screen. He doesn't know the meaning of fear."

She knew her dog. I had no sooner coupled him to the bed leg again than he formed a theory the other dog *was* on the porch, and he made for the door, tugging the bed along. I hauled them both back and would have taken the castors off the bed legs to make it less mobile but they were rusted there for the ages.

After a bit I compromised by barricading the screen door with the cottage's two chairs. This left us only the bed to sit on, but we were happy to find that our combined weights on it slowed Socks down. He could still tow it but not very fast, and it was tiring work on an empty stomach.

After midnight his suspicions and alarms grew less frequent, so that I had need to fall out and shove the bed back to the starting post at only hourly intervals or so.

Off and on during the night Socks also logged time on the remains of his stale bread, and by morning I didn't care much whether or not the motel proprietor knew we had smuggled in a dog. Outside, the Great Dane was no longer in sight, so I took Socks out for his morning gallop.

As we hurtled down the woodland trail, the first person we met, also out for an early stroll, was the proprietor. I reeled Socks in and braced myself for complaints. The man surprised me with a cheery smile. Then he looked at Socks with puzzled interest. "Wish I'd known you had a dog along," he said. "Dogs are welcome here and my dog likes company."

I could think of no reply that would have made me feel the least bit better.

"I'm quite a dog lover, you know," he said, and bent down to examine Socks more closely. "What—ah—breed would you call this one?"

He was probably being tactful, and I'm ashamed to say my reply was no better than a wisecrack. "A bedstead hound," I said. "Fairly rare. I don't imagine you ever heard of the breed."

I was about to spring the small joke, but the motel man took it out of my power. "Oh, I've heard of it," he said, rising from his inspection. "Yes, sir, I've . . . well, heard of it. First time I ever saw one, though." He ran his hand over Socks, who licked it so eagerly that I was sure the proprietor had just come from breakfast.

"Good hunting dog?" he asked, lingering. I said he was a strong and persistent one, and turned to go back to the cottage to get Pat for breakfast.

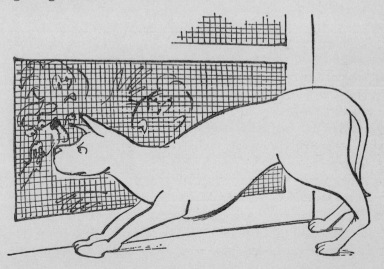

"My Dane's no hunter," the man said. "Wouldn't care to consider selling this one, would you?" he called after me, almost wistfully.

The temptation was nearly overpowering, but it was no way to begin wedded life, I felt. I shook my head. "My wife simply wouldn't hear of it. I'm sorry, but you see, we've had him ever since we were married."

He nodded. "I know how it is. A pet." He paused delicately and then chuckled. "I'll tell you something funny," he said. "Last night I took you two for honeymooners." He gazed again at Socks, who was yanking me off uphill with powerful lunges, and he wagged his head at his own foolishness. "I must have been out of my mind," he said wonderingly.

8

THE ST. LOUIS AD CLUB ZOO

FTER PAT AND I HAD BEEN MARRIED A FEW years, I changed jobs to make more money, and it led to a fresh embroilment with animals. The new job was only indirectly responsible. It was in the advertising department of a utility company; they paid a membership fee for me in the St. Louis Advertising Club, and presently I was asked to edit the club's weekly bulletin. That's what did it. It was a dark day for the members when I agreed.

It was supposed to be a kind of honor, such as standing on the burning deck while everyone else fled, and my boss at the utility company encouraged me into it. "Shows great club spirit," he said. "Won't take much time and you may even get an award or something." He was trying to do a favor, I suspected, for an official of the club who had been told to trap an editor and who had exhausted all other possibilities. This gentleman, whom we'll call Hennessy, doted on the club bulletin and firmly believed that names made news, especially if the name was Hennessy. Well, after all, he was an advertising man.

My boss was wrong about the bulletin not taking much time. It had only four small pages, but when the first press day whizzed around I had accumulated news enough for only two pages. While the printer tapped his foot and kept jerking out his watch, I took care of the third page by devoting it to upcoming program plans, with plenty of white space. Then I paused.

"Now, look, I can't wait all day," the printer said. "How about running the fourth page blank this time?"

I didn't think the club would give me any award for blank pages.

"How about printing COMPLIMENTS OF A FRIEND on it?" the printer said, peering nervously into his pressroom. "That's always good."

I couldn't think of any friends who were that complimentary. In desperation I phoned Hennessy, since he had got me into the fix. I already had one story about him in the bulletin, about a club membership drive he was heading up, but I thought he might be good for another.

He was even better. He filled me in on current business of three or four other committees he was chairman of, on a speech he was giving somewhere, and on celebration plans for his approaching twenty-fifth wedding anniversary. With a light heart I wrote up all these stories and we went to press with flying colors.

When the bulletin came out, it looked surprisingly newsy until you started reading it. Then it seemed to be all Hennessy.

"What in hell is this, the Hennessy Advertising Club?" the club president asked me in a growly interview at that week's luncheon meeting. There were other remarks and a warlike atmosphere wherever I passed. I saw that something would have to be done if I was going to please anybody but Hennessy every week. They should have let me alone. They were better off with Hennessy than with what they got next and from then on. For, as a last resort, I invented a rambling, chatty feature to help fill up space, and in some strange way it immediately became monopolized by animals.

Pat and I had at that time a small Boston terrier named Tux, Socks having passed on to his reward before this time, and I wrote the first column about Tux. He had almost no interest in advertising but he was the only thing that came to mind on the day I sat down to do the column. Just the day before he had barked for the first time in his life. Pat and I had become convinced he couldn't bark at all, but he caught sight of our next-door neighbor's fur coat airing on their clothesline and he took it for a monstrous cat. His bark sounded like muslin ripping, but this was better than nothing, so I wrote it up at some length in the column. Then I sat back to see how the advertising club would take it.

The members seemed a bit bewildered when the weekly bulletin came out, but the tension eased and nobody said anything to my face. This was an improvement over getting squawks about Hennessy, so I wrote about Tux some more the following week. He had accommodated me by making some more small news—he stole and ate a raw tomato intended for a salad. He was the first tomato-eating dog I had known. I made a snappy column out of it and was charmed at how quickly I could fill up space in this fashion and get back to my regular work.

For the next few weeks our Boston terrier was the best advertised dog in the St. Louis area. Then a Newfoundland edged him out of the headlines. The Newfoundland weighed 125 pounds, I estimated, and was lost. He wandered into our back yard looking for something to eat, and I pounced on him. I larded him with Tux's food and wrote up the experience, rich with detail.

By now the ad club members were growing so used to reading more about dogs than about advertising in their publication, they took the Newfoundland in their stride. All over town, advertising men could be seen vaguely scratching themselves as they blinked at the club bulletins that rolled briskly off the press each week.

In the next episode of my serial the Boston terrier came back strong for publicity by attacking the Newfoundland at dinnertime on the back porch. He bit him on the heel, and the bigger dog didn't fight back, I noted. He didn't realize he was being bitten but it made a sporty column. I thought I was all set for several more easy weeks of padding the club paper with my innocent tripe about the dogs. But as usual, the animal world pulled the rug out.

The Newfoundland's owner showed up and claimed him. He told me that the dog's mate had died and that he had then strayed off in a pathetic search for her. In the next week's issue I advised the club membership of this tragic state of affairs and promised to flash them the instant any vital new developments occurred.

None did, and as the next press day approached I was empty of news for the column. I toyed with a notion of even phoning Hennessy for word on his latest doings, but I was saved from it by a bird.

"Oh, say—the dirty robin's back," Pat said when I got home that evening. I had forgotten about him and had never particularly cared for him, but now I fell on him like a starving cat.

"Spring must be here, fellows," I warbled in the ad club bulletin. "We saw the dirty robin in our back yard. He flew to the brim of the fish pool and started taking a bath and then we recognized him." Getting a firm grip on the ball, I ran on for half a page about the robin's bathing habits, or phobia, our theories on its cause and possible effects and so on, until I had wrung the subject dry.

The following week I squeezed out another column on the robin but even I had to admit this one was thinner stuff. The bird lacked the rich, lasting flavor of a Newfoundland, or even of a Boston terrier. I sensed that unless it made news by going mad and committing suicide in the fish pool, the robin was not worthy of my public's time for a third round.

It stayed sane and alive, and I felt myself drifting toward Hennessy once more. He was growing more and more restive over his publicity blackout after the first fine burst, and I was working to avoid running into him alone at the club luncheons in the Hotel Statler. He was a large florid man with a lot of nice prematurely white hair, and he could talk the arm off a slot machine.

The thing that next came to my rescue was, unlikely as it seems, a box tortoise.

"Highway 61, as we call our old garden tortoise, is back," I announced gaily in the next club bulletin. "He had been gone for several months but he has just shown up again." The tortoise, bless him, had not only arrived in the nick, but in such wretched condition that his clinical report alone filled a long column. Probably a truck had run over him, for his shell was cracked on each side where the top and bottom parts joined. I informed the club members that things looked dark, and said I was eager for suggestions on therapy.

None were offered, so I built a ramp with a plank into the back-yard pool, and there the tortoise spent three weeks floating and healing. The progress reports kept the bulletin humming along, and I stretched the story into a five-bagger by devoting one more column to the final week of convalescence on dry land and to the tortoise's returning appetite for melon rinds. Then, cured, he waddled off and left me floundering again.

So far as I could see, I had used up all the material in sight. I was out of dog and tortoise news and I didn't care for more birds short of storks bearing babies. But on totting up I found I had been running the bulletin for seventeen weeks, during sixteen of which it had a strong flavor of fauna. It was uplifting to realize I was a third through with my sentence, and if the club could take thirty-five more weeks of it, I felt I should be man enough to dish it out. Actually, I was getting good co-operation, in a negative way. Ever since I had started giving the members livestock reports in place of Hennessy, I had been let alone. The woman who ran the club office told me I was the most let-alone bulletin editor she could recall since the year one had broken out with pink-eye.

For a few weeks my column had to coast along on trivia—mildly newsy snatches about mice and tropical fish, and one curious item about hogs which I got from our garbage man. The hogs were ones to which the garbage was fed, and they were suddenly living high. For some reason the quality of garbage had zoomed up. This seemed a tantalizing bit of market information for the ad club members to mull over, and I tossed it into the pot. I got only one reaction but it was violent. It came from Hennessy, who could bear his obscurity no longer.

"Birds, turtles, dogs . . . and now *hogs*," Hennessy thundered, cornering me in the hotel lobby after the club luncheon a moment before I could blend into some potted palms. He held a copy of the current club bulletin in his fist and shook it at me. "What the hell we paying for?" he inquired. "The Zoo News?"

This was gross exaggeration. Only my column dealt with such items, even though it did seem to overpower the small publication. But I also ran program notices, committee reports, and such—whatever was offered me, as long as it didn't glorify Hennessy. I would have run the Lincoln-Douglas debates if someone had asked me to.

"Hennessy, I'll just tell you how it is," I said, since it seemed a time for truth. "Personally, I'd love to have you in the bulletin again. You fill it up so. But after the first issue there was talk. I had to kill you for your own good."

Hennessy saw that I was sincere. He gave the matter some

thought. Eventually he hoped to be elected club president and it would not do to antagonize the membership. Just the same he felt injured. "It's been five months, for God's sake," he said, and drew from his inside coat pocket a worn-out copy of my first issue, now virtually in tatters. It still looked like a Hennessy special edition. "I haven't been in the thing since," he said. "Except when I was buried in the middle of some bastard committee."

This was true. Hennessy's recent appearances in print had been official and drab. You could hardly find him with the naked eye.

"It's too bad I'm not a goddam animal," he said bitterly, "or a goddam bird. I guess if I was a goddam swayback trash horse it'd be different."

My ears snapped to attention. "Swayback trash horse? What breed of horse is that, Hennessy?"

"He *hauls* trash," Hennessy said impatiently. "In our suburb. Street sweepings. A Street Department nag with a back shaped like a hammock." There was a brief pause.

"Hennessy," I said, clearing my throat, "you have a nice little story there, and I need a story. Perhaps we could work something out." I felt in all my pockets for note paper. I had none, but Hennessy was tugging at my arm. He motioned toward the Statler bar, just off the lobby. "You can write on a cocktail napkin," he said. "Let's go."

The swayback trash horse made a charming column, a real tear jerker. Hennessy had become emotional as he told me about this patient animal that had to work for a living while shaped like a gravy boat. I took copious notes on several cocktail napkins and when I wrote the thing up I quoted Hennessy, with his permission.

When the bulletin came out, blazing with the horse and Hennessy, I feared a reaction from the ad club members, but there was utter silence. The only comments were from Hen-

nessy who was quite jolly and asked for extra copies, and from the manager of the Society for Prevention of Cruelty to Animals, who phoned to ask if it was a gag. I referred him to Hennessy who, I suspected, had mailed him a marked copy of the bulletin as a good-will publicity gesture.

Well before my deadline for the next issue Hennessy got me on the phone.

"You ever hear of a flower-eating cat?" he asked.

I never had but I was all ears.

"Cat of ours eats my wife's dahlias," said Hennessy. "Siamese cat."

I moistened my lips, wondering how far I could trust Hennessy.

"Honest to God," he said. "I'll take a snapshot of him in the act if you'll use it."

The bulletin's budget couldn't afford any such engraving expense, but Hennessy's offer convinced me of his truth. He and his cat worked up into a pleasant little column. And the following week he had a dog story.

Seemed his wife had been entertaining her club of twenty-four women and she served them some creamed mushrooms —from a batch gathered in the woods by a friend—after she had taken the precaution to offer a sample to the dog. The Hennessy dog had lapped them up so she felt they were all right. But after lunch, one of the guests saw the dog having a fit on the front lawn, and the animal expired before their eyes. A little hysterically, Mrs. Hennessy spilled the mushroom story and called three doctors who came running with stomach pumps. Things were getting under way, with purple-faced women drooping all over the house, when the Hennessy's next-door neighbor hurried over with condolences. "I felt just awful when I saw that car hit your poor dog," she cried. "I was just sick about it."

To spare Mrs. Hennessy's feelings I did not name her, merely crediting Hennessy with relating the story. He was quite happy with the arrangement, and no howls arose from the club members. There was a sense of defeat about them now, I thought, like a man with a tooth that regularly ached once a week.

From then on the bulletin job was a breeze. On the occasional week that Hennessy ran out of animals, I dug some up for the column, but I didn't need many. Hennessy rushed out and bought a new dog, and his wife kept parakeets, and one of their neighbors had kittens, and a baby squirrel fell out of its nest in their yard and became a semiwild pet. The ad club bulletin kept up its lively character, Hennessy walked with a spring in his step, and I attended to my regular work with an easy mind, no longer concerned about my pesky outside chore.

When my year as editor was about up, I even considered volunteering for another, but nobody except Hennessy suggested it. However, word of my availability must have leaked out, because the awards committee took prompt action and presented me with a farewell memento. I heard later that they had quite a tussle over the choice, two members holding out for an engraved dog collar, size fifteen, but this pair was overruled. There was a feeling I might construe such a gift as subtle encouragement to go on, so the committee compromised on the usual presentation—a clock. I heard through the grapevine that the two die-hards tried at the last minute to make it a cuckoo clock, but failed. "Let sleeping dogs lie," they were advised.

9

RATS IN THE CASTLE

SINCE I HAD GONE INTO ADVERTISING, MY FATHER hoped his remaining son would do something he could tell his friends about, and Ted gratified him by taking up doctoring. His studies called for some home experiments, and one of them involved three white rats which he kept in the basement. Pat and I were drawn into it because we were then living in the house, having moved there when my mother died, so Ted could continue his schooling with as little household upset as possible.

Though Pat had not counted on having to live with rats as part of Ted's education, she considered them an improvement over the experiment he had just finished. That one had dealt with fruit flies. He had bred them in the basement in some Mason jars, but they multiplied enormously and then escaped, filling the basement air and gradually working their way upstairs. After Pat had swatted her way around for a few days, she put her foot down. "Science or no science," she told Ted at full volume, "those things have to *go*."

He had been thinking of setting up a maggot colony next, but he changed his mind. He got rid of the fruit flies and brought home the white rats. Seeing that they weren't likely to be flying around her kitchen, Pat agreed to keep an open mind about rats for a while. Since they were all males, she didn't have to worry about their having young, and being white they seemed unratlike to her.

Ted named his rats, to keep his records straight. He called them Whitie, Greenie, and Pinkie, squirting a little colored ink on Greenie and Pinkie to identify them. The rats didn't mind and were good-natured about the whole thing until Ted's experiment got rolling. It dealt with nutrition. Whitie served as the control and got a normal diet, so he stayed happy and docile. Greenie and Pinkie, however, who were being deprived of vitamins, gradually grew more and more grumpy, and took to walking with their backs humped up and casting evil looks toward Whitie's cage.

Presently Pat began to mutter about cruelty to animals. "If you don't start feeding those two," she said to Ted at last, "I will. I can't stand the way they squeak at me."

"They're reacting normally," Ted said, "and please don't go lousing up my experiment."

Pat did not reply, but after a few days I noticed that Greenie and Pinkie were becoming more jolly, and Ted, who was filling a notebook on their nutritional doom, grew suspicious.

"Okay, Pat," he said, a few days later. "You can feed them anything you please. I've got to work at a hospital in Alton for the next month, so I can't be here to look after them for a while."

"You don't say," Pat said. She looked at the rats without enthusiasm.

"Here's the notebook," Ted said. "In case you'd like to continue the experiment." He packed his clothes and went off whistling.

She fed the rats for a few days according to her own ideas, but gradually she grew restive. "I don't know that I care so much about having rats in the basement," she said to me. "Why don't you make a place for them outside?"

There was a small peach tree in the back yard, and I installed the rats on a platform I fixed between the branches.

It was summertime and they seemed to like this arrangement pretty well. At this point a crisis suddenly developed. I came home from the office with some news.

"The boss asked me if I could take my vacation this month," I told Pat. "Next two weeks, in fact. Will that be all right with you?" We were planning merely a leisurely jaunt through the Ozarks, sort of a second honeymoon without Socks, and could go any time.

"Sure—" she said, and stopped. "What about the rats?"

"Dad will be here. Maybe he'll—"

She shook her head, and I had to agree. My father, while he suffered Ted's various experimentings in the interest of education, refused to have anything to do with them personally. He had no use for the rats in particular. "He'd let them starve or worse," Pat said. "I don't think they deserve that."

"We could hire one of the neighbor kids to look after them."

"And get sued?" she cried. The rats were inclined to nip strangers. "The simplest thing to do," she said, "is to stick them in the car and take them along. They're not much trouble."

I felt that even Socks was better than rats on a trip. "You can't sail into a hotel with a cage of rats. They'll throw us out."

"Well, naturally we won't take them *in*," she said. "I thought you knew I meant that. We'll leave them in the car."

She took charge of arrangements and settled on a shoe box for a traveling cage. It seemed a bit cozy for the rats, but they appeared pleased. When the day came for our departure, we put them in it and settled it on the floor of the back seat.

Our destination was, in a general way, the Lake of the Ozarks. This is a sizable body of water made by damming for hydroelectric power and the flooding of valleys over a wide area. There were so many tourist accommodations throughout the region that we could pick and choose. Pat was doing the picking as we rode along, and she picked a lulu. "It's a sort of castle," she said, studying a brochure. "And here's a map to show how to get there."

"A castle? In the *Ozarks?*"

"Well, that's what they say. It's called Ha-Ha-Tonka."

"We're traveling with rats. Can't you find something less elegant than a castle?"

She shook her head. "I'd like to see this place."

I took the route leading to it, and Pat provided diversion by reading the literature out loud. Ha-Ha-Tonka, it seemed, had been built as a private estate by a wealthy Missourian when he retired from business, and was copied from a Scottish castle by imported Scotch stonemasons. Its owner had died before it was quite completed, and the heirs had finished it and were now running it as a resort hotel, American plan.

We turned into the castle's private road and drew up under a massive porte-cochere. The building was small as castles go but big enough to impress us. It was made of stone and set on a mountaintop, viewing the countryside.

We waited, but no one appeared. I started to honk the horn, but Pat shushed me. "Don't do anything crude," she said. We got out of the car and walked up a wide flight of stone steps. They led directly into the great hall, a room as big as two barns, with a fireplace you could have roasted an ox in. A staircase to our left, broad as a highway, led up to a gallery running along three sides of the hall, with room doors opening onto it. "Take off your hat," Pat whispered.

"I don't think anybody's home," I said. "Probably all off hunting for the Holy Grail." My voice resounded hollowly in the vastness, and Pat shuddered.

"Sh-h," she said. "Is that a bell on the counter thing over there?"

I tiptoed over to the thing. It seemed to be a sort of registration desk, and I jingled the bell. After a half-minute a plump young colored boy in an apron appeared at the far right end of the hall and hiked up to us, drying his hands on the apron. "How do—you stayin' or lookin'?" he inquired happily. I had noticed a sign on the desk: "Castle Tour—25¢ Per Person," and I told him we were staying. He opened the register for me to sign, and trotted out to the car for our luggage. I bounded after him. "Not that one," I said, segregating the rat box. "I—ah—keep a spare pair of shoes in the car."

Evidently used to eccentrics, he slapped his leg and led the way in and up the grand staircase to our room, giggling. We seemed to be the only guests in the place, and the room was as big as a house, with a high ceiling, two big closets, a huge and gloomy poster bed, and other furniture in proportion.

"What a perfect setting for a murder mystery," said Pat, who read them and preferred the English-house-party-estate sort.

Our lackey, Alexander by name, spoke up with enthusiasm. "Yes, *ma'am*. That's sure enough part o' the tour." Alexander, I deduced, was the official castle guide.

"You mean to say there was a murder *here?*" I said.

"Long time ago beautiful lady got nailed up by her wicked husband left to poun' the door and starve her poor self to death," Alexander said. It came out in a singsong ribbon without pauses. I felt as if we were taking the tour, and might have felt a chill had not Alexander reeled off his story so cheerily.

"That husband character was worse than Ted," I said when Alexander had left. "Ted only starves rats."

"I wonder if there's anything to the story?" Pat said. We raised the point with the manager of Ha-Ha-Tonka, a Mrs. Haskins, after I had parked the car in a shady place a little later and we had looked over all the downstairs of the castle and its fine view of a waterfall and lakes below.

Mrs. Haskins, a motherly old soul who also cooked the excellent meals, ducked her head. "Well, now," she said. "I don't like to spoil Alexander's story. He's a mighty good worker, and we make a little something out of the tours. But that murder," she added in a lower tone, "—that happened in the *old* castle. The one in Scotland that this one was copied from."

"Much obliged," I said. "Alexander almost had us convinced."

"Giving the tour is much his favorite job," Mrs. Haskins said. "He takes a very personal interest in it. I suppose he isn't exactly truthful, but he almost thinks he is after a while."

"The food is so good and this place is so restful," Pat said the next day, "I think we may as well stay here the whole two weeks." She had pinched a few yeast biscuits from the breakfast table for the rats, and we strolled out to feed them. When we reached the car and discovered what they had been up to, we nearly changed our minds about staying.

I had spread newspapers on the floor in back and let the rats out of their shoe box, but they had made excursions up onto the seat and chewed half a dozen holes in it. "They can't do that!" Pat said.

"Well, they have, and I'll never get the price of seat covers out of Ted. He'd disown the rats first."

"It was a mistake to bring them," she murmured. "But now we've got them, what'll we do?"

"Put 'em in the trunk," I said, but she objected on the ground they might smother, an item I had already thought of.

"I have it," she said. "If we take them up to our room and put them in your hatbox, we can hide it in the spare closet."

"If I'm willing to sacrifice the hatbox, they can stay here in it," I said, but she pointed out that if they escaped from the box they couldn't do any damage in the closet, and were fairly clean little creatures in any case.

It was not a bad plan. Though the hatbox was just cardboard, it was heavy cardboard and the lid fitted snugly. I punched air holes, covered the bottom with shredded newspaper, and the rats were reasonably happy in the box in the closet. Just the same, we didn't stay at the castle nearly as long as we intended.

When we returned from a walk, ready for luncheon, our room had not yet been straightened up. This was one of the chores assigned to Alexander who was not only room clerk and bellboy in addition to tour guide, but also maintenance man, yard man, and chambermaid. He had less need for a leisure-time program than anyone I knew, but since we were the only guests and there had been only one party of tourists that morning, it seemed strange he hadn't got to our room.

"I guess he's been busy maintaining," Pat said. "And isn't that a tour coming up the stairs right now?"

I glanced out and saw Alexander leading a group up the broad staircase. He looked pretty serious. I closed our door part way and winked at Pat. "Let's listen to his patter a minute. I want to hear about the murder in our room again."

To our surprise, Alexander did not pause in front of our door. He scooted right by and halted his customers at another room on the gallery. There he gave them the exact song and dance he had given us about the wicked old man nailing up his beautiful wife in that very room to starve. "He sounds more earnest when he's talking to paying customers," I said, "but I guess he just picks any room that's empty."

Though we saw no more tourists, Alexander still didn't get to our room during the rest of the day. The next morning Pat was preparing to remind him, when Mrs. Haskins made a strange request of us.

"Would you mind if I moved you to number nine?" she

said hurriedly. "It isn't on the corner but it has just as good a view."

We packed up to move ourselves, since Alexander had another party of tourists in tow. He seemed to have become a bit muddled since we had first met him, and we wondered if the strain of juggling all his chores was suddenly beginning to tell. This time the visit to the murder room was pretty brief, and we were amused to notice that it happened to be the room we were moving into, probably because the door was open and it was handy for Alexander to stop there. We moved in as soon as he got his tourists away, and found it almost identical with the room we had been in, and with a spare closet for the rats, too.

We took a drive down to the lakes the next morning, and when we returned to the room we saw that Alexander had been there. But not for very long. "He didn't quite finish making the bed," Pat said as I fed the rats, "and it looks as if he just *threw* the clean towels through the doorway." I picked them off the floor. "I know he's overworked," she said. "But really . . ."

She was considering mentioning it to Mrs. Haskins, but Mrs. Haskins spoke first. "I'm going to have to move you folks to number twelve," she said with a nervous little laugh. "Awfully sorry, but we're having a little trouble with number nine." We said we hadn't noticed anything. "Maintenance trouble," Mrs. Haskins mumbled. "There's always something."

We moved ourselves down the hall to number twelve, a corner room and the duplicate of the first one we had occupied. "This is getting silly," Pat said, unpacking once more. "If the food wasn't so good and I didn't like Mrs. Haskins, I'd vote we march out of here." We still had more than a week if we wished to spend it there, and probably would have worked our way around the gallery through the rest of the

rooms if we hadn't happened to come back to number twelve in midmorning the following day to feed our pesky rats.

Alexander was there, so we loitered on the gallery to give him time to finish. From there we could look down at the great hall, and we noticed that a party of tourists was arriving. "We'd better tell Alexander," Pat said. "He can finish up the bed later."

Alexander wasn't making the bed. He was standing like a moose at bay in the middle of the room, his back to us, a couple of bath towels hung on his arm. From the spare closet there was coming a muffled thumping, familiar enough to us. Ever since their partial starvation during Ted's experiment, Pinkie and Greenie grew quarrelsome when hungry, and as they banged each other against the sides of the hatbox, it acted something like a drum.

Suddenly we heard Alexander speaking, in a husky voice to himself. "Good godalmighty," he quavered, "if I ain't got thisun spooked *too*. The lady poundin' again to get free!" He flung up both his arms, the towels sailed into the air, and he fled out the door without seeing us, and down the gallery, the whites of his eyes showing. We slipped into the room. Pat hurriedly closed the door and shot me a guilty look. I went to the closet and fed the rats, and they quieted down.

I cleared my throat. "On the whole," I said, "I think maybe we'd better—"

"So do I," she said over her shoulder. She had started packing. "I'm afraid we've already ruined the tour for him. You can't enjoy a ghost that co-operates too well."

We fully intended to revisit Ha-Ha-Tonka, without rats, even though Mrs. Haskins was so glad to see us go she almost

cheered. Not long after, however, we read in the newspaper that the castle had accidentally caught fire and was gutted. We couldn't help wondering if Alexander had taken the desperate way out.

10

THE BACHELOR'S CRIMINAL DOG

ONE SUMMER WHILE PAT AND I WERE STILL living with my father and Ted in University City, a kind of madness for back-yard recreation swept through the neighborhood. Somebody in the next block started it by setting up a dwarf golf course in his yard. Then another neighbor made a horseshoe pitch out of his driveway. Shortly after, the fever seized the family next to us on the north, and they slapped a badminton net across their lawn, making life after dark hazardous for anyone taking a short cut, as there were few fences.

"We ought to do something with our yard," Pat said at last. "The Gorsets and ourselves are the only ones out of it." The Gorsets were our neighbors on the south.

"Horseshoes?" Father said. "I used to be pretty good."

She shook her head. She considered horseshoes unladylike. "We ought to be more original."

"Quoits?" Father said hopefully.

"That's practically the same thing. They both get your hands dirty." She looked at me for suggestions, not with much expectation.

"Racing tortoises?" I said. "You make a big circle, put them in the middle, set some lawn chairs around—"

My father and wife turned their backs on me. "Darts?" he said to her. "Shuffleboard? Archery? Bowling green . . . ?"

"A croquet court," she cried. "Nobody else has one."

Father's mouth turned down. "Croquet's a girl's game."

"Well, I'm a girl," Pat said. "But it isn't a sissy game if that's what you mean. Not the way I learned to play it."

He was willing to be convinced, and I didn't care one way or the other. Ted was not consulted because studying medicine was keeping him too busy to vote in household decisions. Father bought a croquet set, read the book of rules, and instructed me on where to pound in the wickets. Meanwhile, Pat was warming up with one of the mallets, and I began to see what she meant about croquet not being a sissy game. An occasional wild practice shot zinged past my legs like a cannon ball, and Father looked more alert.

When I had the court set up, we played a game and she won in a walk. Father, who had had a good eye with a billiard cue, improved rapidly. When the badminton neighbor dropped over, smiling at our little sport, they paired him with me and whipped us stupid. It was a triumph for croquet. Scoffing died aborning. Word got around in the neighborhood that our croquet was murder, and we began to attract visitors. One of them was of particular interest to Pat.

This was a man in his thirties who lived in a neat little house at the end of our street, one of the few with a fenced yard. He was a bachelor, David Kirby, and we knew his dog Duchess, a Doberman pinscher, better than we knew him, having spoken to her through his fence several times. Pat liked the dog and she was simply delighted to get better acquainted with David via croquet. Every housewife in the neighborhood had been toying with ways and means to know him better ever since he had moved in. Each of them had an unmarried sister or cousin or something, and here was a bachelor with a nice house going to waste. But up to this time David and his dog had kept pretty much to themselves.

They ventured up our driveway one evening on a walk. Duchess wasn't in favor of lingering, but David had heard the crack of ball on ball. Presently Pat spotted him peeping at us over a spirea bush. She rushed across the yard with her mallet, nearly frightening him into flight, and said, "We'd love to have you join the game, Mr. Kirby. Hello, baby." The last remark was to Duchess, as David realized after a momentary shock. He said he'd like very much to play, and tied Duchess to our porch banister, to her outrage. They had lived together for three years, and she thought she owned him and didn't care a bit about sharing.

He turned out to be a good player, though the double handicap of being paired with me and of having learned a politer form of croquet than Pat's variety kept him panting. He and I managed to win one game out of four, and Duchess got some satisfaction by grabbing any ball that rolled near the porch and gnawing hell out of it. She had powerful jaws.

"I was sure he'd be a charming man to know," Pat said afterwards. "He's an accountant. That sounds substantial, doesn't it?"

"Very," I said. "Who've you got in mind?"

"Well, there's Gladys. And Louise, and Imogene. And Mary Lou, though he's rather quiet for her—" She glanced at me. "I merely mean he may enjoy meeting some of our friends."

"Your list sounds like a girls' boarding school. He might like to meet a few married couples."

She laughed mirthlessly. "Do you think I'm mad? Those wives would snap him up for their single girl friends. I don't meet many solvent bachelors, you know."

David Kirby became a fairly regular visitor to the croquet court, dragging Duchess along after him, and to lengthen the evenings, Pat had me install a couple of floodlights in the back yard. Now and then she invited an unmarried girl over to play.

I wondered if I ought to warn David that powerful forces

were working against him. His dog certainly knew it. She cut the girls dead. She was a man's dog and she didn't want a woman around. I didn't think David did either, though Pat thought he had walloped Imogene a couple of games with more than passing interest, and he had explained double-entry bookkeeping for ten minutes one evening between rounds to Gladys, who thought a trial balance had something to do with a seesaw.

Pat was thinking of asking these two over again, when David dropped his bombshell. "I wonder if there are any good kennels around here," he said one evening.

"You're going to put Duchess in a *kennel?*" Pat exclaimed.

"Just temporarily," David said. "I'll be away, and—"

"She'll be miserable in a kennel," Pat said. "I know how I'd feel. Why don't you leave her with us?"

David looked surprised and pleased. "I'm sure she'd be happier here." Duchess eyed him suspiciously. She was a terribly intelligent dog and as jealous of him as if she had just found lipstick on his T-shirt.

"And then," Pat said, "you won't have to worry about her. Stay as long as you need to."

David laughed nervously. "Oh, I'll be back in two weeks. The fact is, I'm—um—going off to get married."

Pat stared at him.

"Ah—who's the lucky girl, David?" I asked, wondering if one of Pat's candidates could possibly have slipped him a love potion between games.

"Her name is Laramie," he said, blushing. "Laramie Sparks, back in my home town. I've known her since grammar school."

He left town the next day, dropping Duchess, who had grown gloomy, at our house along with a sack of dog food and a neatly typed list of instructions. Pat received them with better grace than I had really expected, since she had been annoyed at David's skipping off with a strange girl. "Anyway, it's a love match," she confided to me. "That makes up for a lot."

Fall was now approaching, so a general tapering off on back-yard sports set in at this point. The trend caught our neighbor Al Gorset off guard. After thinking it over all summer, Al had fixed on a back-yard project of his own, a swimming pool. This was a much more ambitious thing than anyone else around there had tackled. At that time only movie stars had private swimming pools. Al's wife Madge was not swimming-pool-minded. She wanted to make a rose garden out of the back yard, but Al went ahead with his pool. He had it figured out that if he built a sort of dike around it with the earth he was excavating, he could do it all himself because he would have to dig only half as far down and wouldn't need to have any earth hauled off.

Al dug hard for about a week in his spare time, achieving what my father referred to privately as one hell of a hole, since he had started work at what was to be the deep end of the pool. He was beginning to have second thoughts about his idea, along with calluses, and when a spell of rainy weather came along, he seemed relieved to stop digging for a while and cover the great hole with some old shower curtains laid over clothes poles.

The wet weather also made a problem for Pat. She found it difficult to give Duchess enough exercise, and after a couple of days of sloshing in and out, she turned the dog loose to do her own running.

"What if she runs off?" I said when she told me. "She's so upset about Kirby's deserting her." Duchess was plainly worried, but Pat expected no trouble.

"She just goes exploring around the neighborhood," she said, "but she comes back each time. She's really quite sensible and she does need the exercise."

But Duchess was getting more than exercise out of her jaunts. We found this out a day or two later. "What do you think Duchess brought home?" Pat cried. A bone, I supposed. She led me outside to look under the back porch where the dog was guarding her prize. It was a bunch of artificial grapes, Tokays.

"We'll have to return them, of course," Pat said.

"Go around ringing doorbells to see who's short a bunch of wax grapes?"

"Well, no," she murmured. "Maybe she'll take them back herself when she's tired of them."

Instead, Duchess did it again. "Now she's swiped somebody's good cushion," Pat thundered when I got home from work the next day. So she had—a nice canvas-covered one in royal blue. "Those things cost money," Pat said. "I think it came off a glider. We'll have to—"

I shook my head. Duchess had the cushion and grapes tucked in a far corner under the porch, where they got only a little wet from the off-and-on rain. "Let Kirby return the stuff when he gets back," I said. "She's his thief."

Pat tried keeping the dog indoors for a day, but when she was let out for a run in the late afternoon she disappeared and came back an hour later dragging with difficulty an umbrella, the large kind that fits into an outdoor table.

"And now she's got herself a gazing globe," Pat cried, the following day. The thing was as big as a basketball, and slippery. Apparently she had rolled it home with her nose.

"I think she wants me to put today's treasure on the porch for safekeeping," I said. "See how she's looking at me?"

"I'll porch her," Pat exclaimed, shaking her finger at Duchess. "Do you know what I'm going to have to do now? I'm going to have to hide all these things somewhere till David Kirby gets back. What if the owners come around looking for them. Do you think they'll ever believe a *dog* did it?"

This was sound reasoning, no doubt, but it was a mistake

to say it in front of Duchess. She may not have understood all the words but she caught onto the tone, and she was a dog of decision. When Pat prepared to stow the swag, it was gone, nor could we find it in the garage or in any secret spots under the yard shrubbery. "Maybe she's gone straight and has taken it back," I said, but my wife scoffed.

"All I hope," she said, "is that she's hidden it somewhere in David Kirby's yard. It'd serve him right."

She had not, but we didn't find it out until that Saturday night, and the discovery was preceded by such an uproar as the neighborhood had not experienced since the time the River Des Peres had backed up during a cloudburst and drowned three blocks of basements.

This Saturday night was also rainy, in a drizzly nagging way—the way it had been all week. Consequently Duchess was still taking her exercise on her own, though she had displayed no more trophies to us. Al Gorset next door hadn't been able to get back at his swimming-pool digging in the wet weather, and there was speculation on whether Al could even get the thing finished in time for a skating rink.

"She's got a smug look on her face," Pat said of Duchess when she returned from her before-bedtime run that night. "I'll bet she's been up to something."

Duchess had an innocent "Who—me?" look. "I'd give a pretty penny to know where she's stashed those things," Pat said. "You know what I think? I think she knows David Kirby has a girl, and she's hoping to win him back with gifts. She's just plain jealous."

"Very likely. Socks was jealous of me when we were married."

She smiled. "Naturally. But at least he was law-abiding. With this criminal around you don't know what to expect next."

Certainly we didn't expect to be awakened a couple of

hours after midnight by a horrid crash from outside. And though it wasn't Duchess's crash, for she was in the basement, she certainly complicated it by something she had secretly been doing, we discovered.

Pat woke up first, as usual. She sprang out of bed, rocking it like a tub in a tidal wave, and pressed her nose against the screen in our upstairs bedroom window, which she flung open.

"The owls again?" I said into the pillow. She was infatuated with a pair of little owls that sometimes sat on our telephone wire at night.

"Owls?" she whispered. "I think it's elephants!"

The nearest elephants were in the zoo in Forest Park, perhaps three miles away, and they were in cages. I joined her at the window.

"I think it came from the Gorsets' yard," she said. "Do you see anything?"

"Only Al's swimming pool— Hey! The cover's gone." I looked harder. "And Al's *in* it."

My father rapped at our bedroom door, and Pat leaped into a robe and admitted him. "For the Lord's sake," he said to me. "You fall out of bed again?" Ted occasionally fell out, too, but he was on night duty that evening, at a hospital.

I pointed out the window. "It's Al Gorset. Gone swimming."

Father rushed to the window. He could see like a cat in the dark. "Not enough water in that hole to swim," he said. "That isn't Gorset, either. That's a horse."

We all pulled on some clothes and hurried downstairs and outside, turning on our croquet floodlights. Al Gorset was already out in his yard, in pajamas and slippers, waving a flashlight at his swimming pool. Madge was running after him with a raincoat, for it was still drizzling lightly. The horse in the hole had begun neighing in a hysterical tenor as if he thought his hour had come. As the uproar continued, other neighbors, their flashlights glimmering like lightning bugs, were hastily picking their way across lawns.

Al looked hopeful when he saw my father. Father was old enough to remember something about horses. "What do you say to a horse to make him jump out of a hole?" Al yelled in between neighs.

Father frowned down at the horse, a runty specimen none of us had ever seen in the neighborhood. "Giddy-ap!" he roared. The horse laid its ears back and neighed over its shoulder at him. "He's lamed," Father said flatly. "Probably stuck in the mud, too." The other neighbors slithered around the diked edge of Al's pool, playing their flashlights on Al's victim and now and then on Al, when suddenly one of the women in the crowd let out a whoop and pointed downward into the hole.

"*There* it is," she shrieked. "My good glider cushion!"

Pat and I craned our necks. The cushion which Duchess had dragged home, its royal blue muddied but defiant, lay in Al Gorset's swimming hole, in the oozy bottom.

"Why, look," another lady cried at her husband, her flashlight beam boring into Al's excavation. "Isn't that our terrace umbrella, Richard?"

Her husband, a ruddy man weighing approximately 220, teetered on the dike and peered downward at where the horse had the umbrella anchored. "Damned if it isn't," he said. "Get your horse's foot off it, Gorset," he added to Al, who was as surprised as anybody over the contents of his swimming pool.

Before Al could answer, still another neighbor housewife spoke up, having just recognized, as had Pat and I, the gazing globe floating in the puddle amidships of the horse's hind and forelegs. "So this is what happened to it," she said, glaring across at Al. "I suppose it got off its pedestal and rolled down here all by itself?"

"Honest, Mrs. Starbright," Al said, "I don't know any more

about this than the man in the moon." The lady sniffed loudly, and Pat pinched me.

"Do you see the grapes anywhere?" she whispered. I didn't, though there were several mysterious lumps under the shower curtains, which the horse had carried down with him in his plunge. "I think you'd better tell them," she said into my ear, but I was delayed from doing so by a new arrival, two of them. They were a pair of University City policemen in a scout car. They roared up the driveway we shared with the Gorsets and jumped out as if they smelled dinner, but they halted at the edge of Al's swimming pool and stared. The horse had stopped neighing and just rolled its eyes at the policemen.

"Is that a horse, Eddie?" one muttered to the other.

Eddie scratched his jaw. "Say, who's in charge here?"

"Well, it's my place," Al said, "but—"

"Can't keep horses in residential section, mister," Eddie said. "There's a zoning law."

"I'm not keeping him," Al said, rather plaintively. "I wish he'd go away. He's ruining my swimming pool."

"Swimming pool?" said the policemen together.

"It isn't quite finished," Al said, "but as soon as this rain stops—"

"You got a permit?" asked the policeman who wasn't Eddie.

"I'm not running a business," Al said. "This is a private back-yard pool."

"There's a building code," said the policeman.

"Code be damned," said the large ruddy neighbor suddenly. "What about our umbrella?" He pointed, and the policeman looked. "And our gazing globe," cried the lady who had lost it. "And my good cushion," cried the glider lady.

Eddie pointed his flashlight at poor Al, who had so frank and open a countenance that I didn't see how anybody could suspect him of anything. "What's these people's stuff doing in your swimming pool, mister?" Eddie said. He sounded more puzzled than anything, but I guess Al had had enough.

"What's it doing here?" he yelled, his voice cracking. "Waiting till I get enough to open a secondhand shop, I guess."

"Oh, for pity sakes, Al," said Madge Gorset.

My father, suddenly realizing he was standing out in the rain, gave Al a disapproving stare and stalked off home.

"Well," Eddie said uncertainly, looking Al up and down. The policemen weren't used to arresting residents. They seldom arrested anybody, but under these circumstances I was afraid they might feel duty-bound to clap Al in the pokey. I tapped Eddie on the shoulder, causing him to jump and try to find his gun.

"I think I can clear this whole thing up," I said, and I told on Duchess. It was surprising how willing everybody was to believe the worst of her.

"In view of this," the ruddy man said to Al, "I apologize for what I was thinking, Gorset. But just the same, what about our umbrella? It's still in your hole."

Al got a garden rake from his garage but he couldn't fish out the umbrella. The horse wouldn't get off it, and the umbrella looked bent. Al enticed the gazing globe up the side of the pool, but that was all he could recover. While he was at it, Eddie the policeman thought of a way to rescue the horse. "Start shoveling this dirt back in," he said, "so's he'll have something to climb up on." Al sighed and got a spade from his garage. He started pitching earth back into the hole, burying the rest of Duchess's loot and also burying the horse up to the knees. The horse took it hard and started neighing hoarsely again until it pulled its feet loose and discovered it was rising to freedom by inches.

Al had to shovel in about half the earth before the horse was able to lurch up out of the hole and go limping off with the law. "I'll dig your stuff out later, folks," Al said, leaning on his spade and panting. "When I get back to work on my swimming pool."

The ruddy man gazed down into the half-filled hole and voiced an opinion that had become pretty general. "Oh, the hell with it," he said. "Let's all go back to bed."

The rainy spell ended that night, allowing us to keep Duchess on a leash for legal exercise for the duration of her stay, but Al Gorset didn't finish his swimming pool. His wife hired a man to rush some topsoil to fill the hole to the brim and haul away the clay Al had dug out, and she had three dozen hybrid teas planted there before Al could say a word. He didn't seem to mind much, though, until David Kirby came home and Al met the bride. Laramie was as cute as a shirtful of kittens. She could have jammed traffic dressed in potato sacks, and Al looked sad. "You know," he said, "this neighborhood *needed* a swimming pool. Maybe next year—" Madge gave him a look, and he changed the subject.

When David brought Laramie over to meet us and to get Duchess, the dog remained sitting and regarded him coolly. He seemed startled. "She always jumps all over me when I get home," he said. "Has she been all right?"

"Physically, yes," Pat said.

"She looks perfectly lovely," Laramie exclaimed. "I do adore nice big dogs." Duchess gave her a surprised stare.

"She's a moral bankrupt, Dave," I said. "Tried to swipe everything loose in the neighborhood." I detailed the jobs she had pulled, and he was shocked.

"Good Lord—I never knew her to do anything like that before," he exclaimed. "See here, young lady—" he said to Duchess, who was giving him hard, defiant looks.

"Don't you dare to scold her, Dave," Laramie cried. "It was a perfectly natural thing to do." All four of us pivoted to her. "She was just upset with you gone," Laramie said. "I think it was very touching."

Instantly Duchess got to her feet. She stalked right by David and over to his bride, who was sitting on our sofa. As Laramie smiled at her, Duchess climbed up into her lap, nearly crushing her, and settled down. The marriage, we saw clearly, was going to prosper.

11

"NO PARTIES, NO PETS"

RS. NIGGLE SAYS SHE WANTS THE APARTMENT back," Pat cried. "Now what?" I removed my Navy cap and coat, sidled into the tiny living room of the duplex apartment we were subleasing in southeast Washington, and considered the matter. World War II was on. It seemed I would be stationed here while it lasted, and we had hoped the sublease would last, too.

I phoned a man who kept in touch with vacancies as a favor to Navy people—the same one who had found the sublease for us six months before. "I can't even find a vacant dollhouse now," he told me. "Have you tried Baltimore?"

"Baltimore, *Maryland?*" I said.

"Closer than Philadelphia, and there's an early morning train. You wouldn't have to get up much before five."

I thanked him and passed the news to Pat. "I haven't anything against Baltimore," she said, "but that's an awful lot of railroading just for a place to sleep. Let's try an ad in the paper here first." She turned to the FURNISHED RENTALS WANTED column of the evening paper and read the ads there carefully. "All wrong," she said, and borrowed a pencil from me. "Now. If we owned a home here and decided to rent it, what would we want first of all?"

"Money."

"*First* of all, we'd want it looked after. We'd want responsible people and we'd want them to stay." She rapidly wrote her ad:

Midwestern home owners here for duration.
No parties, no pets, no nonsense.

"I guess so," I said when she read it to me. "We own a home" (or at least we were paying for one we had bought in a suburb of St. Louis before we left), "we're probably here for the duration, we haven't thrown any parties so far, and at the moment we have no pets. I don't know about the no-nonsense bit."

"That's to inspire confidence," she said. "It means anything they like to everybody who reads it."

It must have, because we got a great lot of answers. Most were offers to share a home with us or rent out a room with kitchen privileges, but two owners offered their homes intact. "One's a Georgetown mansion, $350 a month," Pat reported, "and the other's—"

"Let's look at the other," I said. It was, she told me, a cottage in Arlington, Virginia, just across the Potomac.

"A Mrs. Mothersill," she added. "Her husband's going into the Seabees and she's going to live with her sister in Alexandria. She said we sounded lovely."

We took the bus over and found it was a spic-and-span five-room cottage with a fireplace, in a neighborhood of small homes. "And there's all kinds of firewood," said Mrs. Mothersill, taking us into the back yard. She was a capable, no-nonsense type of woman.

"Wood?" I looked all around a decaying stump for it until I realized the stump was what she meant.

"That 'no pets' in the ad was what caught my eye," she said in a confidential tone.

"We didn't mean we're down on pets—" I began, to keep the record straight, but Pat backed up on my feet.

"No pets, no parties," she said firmly. Mrs. Mothersill patted her cheek, and we rented the place, ninety dollars a month. Our landlady said she had just turned down a couple who offered a hundred dollars but had a tabby cat and looked, she said, as if they drank. We moved in the following week and didn't see Mrs. Mothersill again for a couple more, when she showed up at a very awkward moment.

Meanwhile we had got acquainted with the neighbors on each side. Those on the west were the Ashleys, about our own age. To beat the meat shortage they were raising chickens in a shed Ashley built from kindling. He had no car and had carried the kindling home in such tremendous loads that he walked down the middle of the street, and passing trucks treated him as an equal.

An old Dutch couple lived on the other side. Their name was Kuyper and they gardened every inch of their small yard so intensively they practically lived off it. We were planning to buy a farm after the war, so we studied their system through the fence, and when they noticed us they apologized for speaking Dutch to each other and to their dog, a little whisk broom named Gail. I tried English on her, and she looked blank. "She doesn't gr-r-r-asp it," said Mr. Kuyper tolerantly. He was in government service as an interpreter and juggled seven or eight languages. "Anyway, she doesn't like men," he said, "I included."

It was a remark he lived to repent. Just to be contrary the little beast took a fancy to me as well as to Pat, and it almost got us thrown out of our new house.

Each Wednesday evening Mr. and Mrs. Kuyper attended a Theosophical Society meeting. They had to leave Gail at home and it worried all three of them. "Why not leave her with Ken and me?" Pat suggested when she learned of this. "We like dogs and we miss having one of our own." They left her with us the next Wednesday evening, and everybody was satisfied except Gail. Even when she was happy she looked bothered, and now she seemed to think she was being sold down the river. I couldn't comfort her in Dutch so I put her on my lap and it reminded me of something. I had told Mrs. Kuyper I'd trim Gail's claws. Whenever the Kuypers did it, both of them became nervous wrecks and Gail went to pieces, so they had been putting it off.

Pat brought our toenail clippers, and Gail began to squirm on my lap. "I'll take a little off tonight," I said, "and some more in a week or two when the quick recedes. Let's hope she doesn't bite."

She didn't bite but at the first clip she belted out a howl that jingled the light fixtures. The paring rattled down on the hearth. "Not so much," Pat cried.

"I didn't hurt her," I roared over Gail's howling. "She's a hypochondriac." I clipped again, fetching a series of yelps ending in a bloody-murder shriek. She held it for six beats, and when she stopped we noticed a rapping at the front door.

"The Ashleys probably think we're balancing our budget," Pat murmured, and opened the door.

It was not the Ashleys. Our landlady was standing on the porch, mouth open, eyes wide.

"How nice of you to drop by, Mrs. Mothersill," Pat said after a moment of meditation. "Come in—we aren't doing a thing." She did so rather warily, staring at Gail wriggling on my lap.

"This isn't our dog, of course," I said, setting her on the floor. "We're just—" Gail made a mad dash for Mrs. Mothersill and protection and tried to climb her legs.

"SHEE-OO!" cried our landlady, flapping her skirt and hopping. Gail fled to the sofa and made it in one leap. Pat snatched her off. "It's the Kuypers' dog," she said hastily. "We're merely keeping her."

"*Keeping* her?" Mrs. Mothersill exclaimed. The phrase, "no pets," seemed to shimmer in the air. Mrs. Mothersill darted a glance at her good sofa.

"Just for the evening," Pat said, brushing dog hair off. "She's the Wednesday evening dog. Do sit down."

"I'm terrified of dogs," Mrs. Mothersill muttered, tenderly feeling her legs. "I just dropped by to pick up that little blanket chest in the bedroom. I'm going to have it refinished." I went back to the bedroom to get the chest, in which I had been keeping cigars and a bottle of whisky, and toted it out to our landlady's car. She drove off, a bit jerkily.

"I'm sure she got a runner in those stockings," Pat said. "Could you get her a pair at Ship's Service?" I said I'd keep an eye out, and not long after that I spotted some and bought Mrs. Mothersill a pair, guessing at her size.

Pat phoned her about it to help cheer her, and Mrs. Mothersill said she'd pick the stockings up Thursday evening when she brought back the chest, now refinished. "Thank heaven it isn't tonight," Pat said on Wednesday evening. "We're not only sitting with a dog this time—we're sitting with a sick chick."

"You're not fooling me," I said. "Ashley wouldn't ask us to mind one of his sick chicks. He'd wring its neck." Ashley had some weaklings in his current flock, I knew, and he culled them with an iron hand.

"He was going to," said Pat, "but Mrs. Kuyper begged him to let her have it for a pet. Well, she did. And she was going to nurse it and miss the Theosophical meeting tonight. And she's been nice to us, and I felt sorry for her. . . . And stop looking at me like that. It's only for one evening."

The Kuypers brought the chick and Gail by on their way to the meeting. It was a runty half-grown chick, bedded down in a bushel basket and clacking morosely. "I'm going to park it on the front porch," I told Pat when they had left. "The weather's warm enough, and I can hear it just as well from out there if it takes a turn for the worse."

It didn't, but our luck did. Mrs. Mothersill got mixed up on her dates and arrived shortly after. She skidded to a stop when she saw what was on her front porch and stayed outside on the front walk. "It's not our chick, Mrs. Mothersill,"

Pat cried, rushing out. "We're just minding it." Gail came strolling out onto the porch and waved her tail at the landlady. "We're minding her again, too," Pat said. "It's Wednesday. We were expecting you Thursday."

The chick clacked gloomily, and Mrs. Mothersill backed off, her face working. I fetched the refinished chest from her car and lugged it into the house through the back door. "Your nylons!" I heard Pat screeching as I returned through the living room. She was running out after Mrs. Mothersill, who was legging it for her car.

"Well," Pat said, coming back from her mission, "I was going to ask about getting us a more practical dining table, but now I just hope she doesn't give us notice."

We were making do with a small Duncan Phyfe style of table too delicate for everyday use, but rather than arouse Mrs. Mothersill further, we bought ourselves a sturdy old round table at a secondhand store and I painted it sage green.

The summer went along without further visits from Mrs. Mothersill, who seemed to have taken the stand that what she didn't know couldn't hurt her. However, except for Gail on Wednesday nights we had no pets. But when cool fall weather came, fate stepped in again.

After we had burned the old stump in the fireplace, Pat phoned a cordwood dealer. "Bring you a load in a couple of weeks," he said. "Thirty dollars." She dropped into a chair we kept near the telephone for such occasions and told him not to bother. She had been thinking of spending ten dollars at the most.

There was some wooded land near by, perhaps a dozen acres, and we had a look. It was littered with dead limbs fallen to the ground, so we made a sledge out of one, loaded it with others, and dragged it off. After the first hundred yards down the street, we were blowing like factory whistles and scandalizing the neighborhood, but the excitement made a big hit with one resident, a huge dog with long brownish hair. She followed the sledge, happily grabbing hold and tugging east when we were going south, and south when we turned west.

"I'm going to run this crazy animal home," I said, stopping to pant, but Pat said the dog was trying to help.

"Besides, she's pretty," she added. "Here, Beauty."

It was a triumph of flattery. Beauty was so pleased with the name, she licked a couple of innocent bystander dogs we passed and came all the way home with us. We didn't ask her in, but Pat made her a baked-bean sandwich and it cemented the love affair. Every day after that, Beauty accompanied her up to Columbia Pike, three blocks away, where Pat did her shopping. My wife was touched by the attention, and it gave her an idea when she saw that the finish of our new green table was showing some wear in spots.

"Instead of repainting the whole thing, you can just decorate the worn places," she said. I had once free-handed an ivy vine, unknown to botany, on a kitchen-chair back, and she considered me a practical artist. "Paint some pictures of Beauty on the table," she said. "One on each of the worn spots."

There were four of them, where we rested our arms. From ivy to Beauty seemed an easy step. I snipped some long hair from her flank when she dropped by for a bean sandwich, and made a passable small brush, though I had to paint her in a sitting pose to avoid fine detail. I gave her an extra-bushy tail to make up for it. Pat thought it a good resemblance and as an afterthought had me do a pine-cone border around the table edge with the paint that was left. The border had nothing to do with Beauty, but the paint happened to be the approximate color of pine cones.

As if to reward us for this kindness to animals, we were sent by a friend in the Midwest a windfall of ration-book red points at this time. They were on the brink of expiring, and though Pat thought it was probably illegal, she dashed right up to the Pike with them and came home bearing a whole ham. She had never before had enough points to squander, and to ease her conscience she invited Mrs. Mothersill over to a ham dinner for the following day.

"We owe her something," she explained to me, "since she was nice enough to overlook our keeping Gail, not to mention that ridiculous chick episode."

"And we haven't once allowed Beauty in the house."

"And we aren't going to," she said. "She's suddenly taken up with a whole gang of dogs. They all followed me home from the store today." I assumed the ham had been the attraction, but not so. It was Beauty's time to become breedable. We didn't realize this, but for the moment Beauty was one of the biggest attractions in Arlington County.

When I got home the next day shortly before the time we were expecting Mrs. Mothersill, the kitchen smelled wonderful. I set a fire of our salvaged wood to blazing on the hearth in the living room, and when our landlady arrived we all had a swig of grape juice there, the strongest drink we felt it safe to offer. It seemed to reassure Mrs. Mothersill. "I feel right at home," she said, settling back a bit from the edge of her chair.

"You know," Pat said, "this is the very first party we've given, if you can call it a party."

"No parties," I said, "no pets." We were all tittering merrily when Pat, who was sitting nearest the dining-room doorway, suddenly froze.

"Something burning?" I asked.

"No—I thought I *heard* something—" she said, jumping to her feet and starting for the kitchen. I dashed after her, and Mrs. Mothersill skittered back to the edge of her chair.

Pat stopped short at the kitchen entrance, and I ran into her. She spun around and clapped one hand over my mouth, stifling a yell. Beauty was standing in the middle of the kitchen, inhaling ham aroma. Pat started to chase her quietly out the back door, which she had pushed open to enter.

It was too late. Beauty's admirers were hot on her trail. The whole pack boiled up the back-porch steps, yawping and giving the show away. Clutching her grape juice, our landlady came bounding around the corner from the living room.

I got ready to catch her. If the sight of a small dog such as Gail could terrify her, I thought Beauty would finish her off. But I hadn't counted on the housekeeper in her. It was stronger than fear. She banged her glass of grape juice down on the green dining table and dived past us into the kitchen. Grabbing up the first thing that came to hand—a floor mop— she belabored Beauty. "You get right out of my kitchen," she cried. "You great hairy thing." Beauty departed, howling, sweeping her entourage off the porch in front of her. Before you could say "dog lover" they were all gone. Mrs. Mothersill, somewhat winded, replaced the floor mop, and Pat started to explain that she had left the kitchen door slightly ajar to air the place, and so . . .

"Why, it wasn't your fault, dear," Mrs. Mothersill said, amazing us. "It was that thing they call Floozy."

"F-Floozy?" Pat said.

Mrs. Mothersill shuddered. "That big dog. She's the one that always used to come smelling around my garbage can till I threw a pan of hot water on her one day."

"I—didn't know you knew her," Pat murmured, and then suddenly stiffened. Mrs. Mothersill, returning to the green dining table for her grape juice, was staring at my four likenesses of Beauty, or Floozy.

"Did *you* do this?" she cried at Pat.

"I did," I said glumly.

"Mercy sakes," said our landlady. "It's perfectly lovely."

Pat and I exchanged blank looks. "You . . . *like* it?" she faltered.

"Love it," Mrs. Mothersill declared. "It's so primitive." She hesitated. "I wonder if you'd consider selling this table to me when you leave—?"

Pat drew a deep breath. "Mrs. Mothersill—you can *have* it when we leave. If you're really sure you want it."

"Want it! Why, I adore squirrels," said our landlady. She patted one of Beauty's portraits lovingly. "And an acorn border," she said, patting the pine cones. "Perfect combination."

I poured us all another bumper of grape juice. "It's a pleasure to give it to you, Mrs. Mothersill," I said. "You know, I had a feeling you'd recognize the decoration."

12

ROMANTIC HEIFERS

SOME FRIENDS OF OURS WHO OWNED A PART-time farm had a chilling habit of naming their cattle for people we all knew. "Agnes is putting on a lot of weight lately," they would remark, and my wife would make sympathetic noises.

"Oh, the poor thing," she'd exclaim. "And right after she bought that lovely beige gabardine suit, too." This would produce a one-sided laugh, the Agnes mentioned being a six-hundred-pound Hereford cow.

"Gene's looking good," they might say, and before I could agree that his color was better and his hair had stopped falling out so fast, they would add that they planned to butcher him in a month.

When Pat and I bought a farm of our own after the war, as planned, a forty-acre place southwest of St. Louis, we carefully avoided this quaint practice for the good of our nerves. When we bought four black Angus steers of varying sizes to raise for beef, we named them Eenie, Meenie, Miny, and Moe. We didn't know anybody by those names and we didn't plan to meet any. Soon after, we found that owning four handsome steers presented other peculiar hazards, no matter what their names were. Our education was unwittingly arranged by a week-end neighbor.

He was Thad Burton and he owned the place just in back of ours. We shared the entrance road, a semipublic lane, and he and his wife Maggie regularly stopped to say hello on the weekly trips to their farm. Strictly speaking it was not a farm, though they did have some open land in grass.

Thad was an artist and when he caught sight of our steers for the first time he saw them with an artist's eye. "Wow," he said, "what gorgeous steaks. What gains do you expect they'll make?"

I said I hoped they'd average fifty pounds each a month and justify the fortune we had spent improving the pastures.

Thad drooled. "Think of that. Every month you'll be converting mere grass into two hundred pounds of beef without a lick of work. Pretty soft."

I already had enough acquaintance with cattle to expect some work but I let the remark ride. Thad was not ordinarily a dreamer, but cattle were outside his experience so far.

On their way back to town the next day the Burtons stopped again. The steers were lined up along the garden fence, hoping for a handout, and Thad blinked hungrily at them. "Think I could buy some where you got yours?" he asked. "We've got a lot of good pasture going to waste."

There were no more of the Angus available, but I was sure he could buy some kind of steers. "But who'll look after them when you're not here?" I said.

He seemed surprised at the question. "Why, they'll look after themselves. There's a spring they can drink at. Grass and water—what else can they want?"

Steers occasionally wanted something else, I knew, such as freedom and hell-raising. But the cattle Thad bought a week later wanted even more. They were not steers at all, but young lady cows, and romance was flashing in their wide brown eyes.

The big stake truck that brought them was trailing Thad's station wagon up our lane. Thad, who had come without Maggie this time, paused at our front-yard fence, and the truck lumbered to an uneasy halt behind him. It seemed alive with heifers and it took a heavy list to port as they crowded over to peek through the stakes at our steers in the offing. The steers, separated by the width of our yard and garden, were gawking back through the fences.

"How do you like 'em?" Thad called to Pat and me. He waved his left arm backward in the direction of his livestock, a lordly gesture. Already he had the air of a cattle baron.

"They—they're very pretty," said Pat, who could be tactful when she chose. One of the heifers mooed prettily at our steers. Their spokesman, Miny, blatted back, sending a thrill of excitement through the truck.

"Pretty my hind leg," I said. "They're heifers, Thad."

"Sure. Five head," he said, staring at me as if I had said they were wolves. "Average about three hundred pounds each. The lot cost me $380. Heifers, steers—what's the difference? Both beef, aren't they?"

"We better get going," the truck driver yelled, eying our steers, "before something happens."

"Check your fences," I called at Thad as he started off. "Especially your east one."

His east fence was also our west one, and we informally maintained it between us. "I think you'd better check it, too," Pat said to me as the caravan trundled away. "Those heifers look pretty lively."

I wasn't much of a fence fixer. I usually prevailed upon some softhearted farmer neighbor to do it for me, but that took negotiations and this seemed an emergency. I got a claw hammer, filled my pockets with staples, and set off across the fields to our west line in back. Falling into step, the steers all paraded along with me. So far, they had been easygoing animals, placidly grazing. According to my weight tape they had already gained eighty pounds among them in a couple of weeks. I had got the tape for ten cents from the Purina feed company. You circled a steer's ribs with it just behind the shoulders and read off his approximate weight, if he was willing.

At the southwest corner of the west fence the steers stopped when I did, and formed a fascinated clump, heads together, studying my technique with hammer and staples. Cattle are very nosy. The fence was about five feet high, with four strands of barbed wire, none of them any too tight. I immediately discovered I should have brought another claw hammer to pull up slack in the wire while I drove staples. Three hands would have been nifty, too.

As I was looking around for a stone to use as a second hammer, I noticed that all four steers had suddenly come to attention, heads in the air and ears cocked. From the Burton side of the fence a great crashing approached us through the woods. A few seconds later the heifers zoomed out into the open, instantly followed by Thad in full cry, waving a hammer.

The heifers skidded to a halt at the fence. Suddenly shy, they looked coquettishly at the steers, who seemed astounded at this bit of luck. Thad staggered forward, panting. "Shoo," he said hoarsely to his heifers.

"Let's tighten the damn fence," I said, "before they jump it."

"Jump it?" Thad said as we began wire-stretching and hammering, a job he was much better at than I. "Have your steers been getting out?"

"I was speaking of your heifers."

"Oh, well, they won't jump it," he said, "if your steers don't encourage them."

We worked along for a piece, each of us accompanied by his herd, which were nuzzling through the fence. "See what I mean?" Thad said.

I had already hammered my thumb several times. "*No*-body has to encourage flirty heifers," I said. "Why did you have to get mixed up with girl cows?"

Thad sternly took up some slack in a wire. "Good fences make good neighbors," he said.

I hit my thumb again as we finished the job. The steers were still mooning through the fence at the heifers, and I had to break off a dogwood switch to drive them back to the barn lot ahead of me. On his side I could hear Thad switching at his heifers, which were bounding all over his woods.

"Poor Thad's being run ragged," I said to Pat when I got back. "The fellow who sold him those heifers isn't doing his heart any good."

Thad looked pretty worn when he stopped by on his return to town the next afternoon, Sunday. He had spent the time going over the rest of his fences and chasing the heifers. "You feeling better?" he asked me.

"I'm feeling sorry for you," I said. "You bought yourself a problem, Thad."

"Oh, they were just a little skittish," he said. "They've calmed down now. They're as gentle as rabbits."

If Thad's heifers were like rabbits, it was jackrabbits. Bright and early Monday morning they jumped the fence we had tightened and looked up the steers, which were obediently grazing our front pasture. The steers immediately forgot all about duty and gave themselves over to frolic. I had already left for my job in town, and Pat, who had chased cattle and learned her limitations, didn't try it. She decided she'd ignore the whole thing till I got home.

But presently she took a harder look at the high jinks going on in the pasture and changed her mind. The heifers were skipping about, followed by our lumbering, low-slung steers. Now and then a heifer would float over a cross-fence like a bit of fluff, and a pursuing steer would try to follow her, and carry the fence down with him. When Pat saw our posts snapping off and the fences tumbling right and left, she rushed to the phone and shrieked for help.

She called Gus Brinkmeyer. He was our nearest neighbor and had two strapping sons in their teens, Lew and Dick. The boys came over and sent the heifers kiting home. They regarded cattle chasing as a pleasant recess in the day's work. Pat, breathing faster from the mere thought of it, phoned me at the office with a dramatic report, and I phoned Thad Burton.

"You and your 'rabbits,'" I said.

"What rabbits?" Thad said.

"Your heifers. They've been busting fences all over our place." I filled him in.

"My gosh. Where are they now?" he asked.

"Ten minutes ago they were home again," I said. "That's the latest flash."

Thad groaned. "I can't get out there again till Saturday. Would you ask Gus and the boys to raise our joint fence by another strand?"

"Be delighted to."

"And have them fix your busted fences too," Thad said. "I'll pay for it, of course."

When I got home Pat reported that the heifers had made a return call at noon and had been scooted back home again by the Brinkmeyer boys. I phoned Gus, who nearly hung up when he heard my voice. "Listen," he hollered, "my whole day's been broke up by—"

"I'm calling for Thad Burton, Gus," I said. "Can you do some fencing tomorrow?"

"Well, now, after a day like this I don't see how—" Gus began, but I broke in.

"I just looked out the window, Gus. Here they come again," I said. "All five of them, running like deer."

"Oh, godalmighty," Gus said, gurgling it into the telephone. "Me and the boys'll be there in the morning. Leave 'em be for the night."

By morning the steers were dragging, but the heifers looked fresh as the dew. A disquieting thought came to Pat and me at the same moment. "Those steers seem kind of skinny all of a sudden," she said.

"All chasing and no grazing. They won't make any gains that way." I made a mental note to slip the weight tape around them as soon as I got home that evening, but when I got home I found the steers had just left home.

"They're over at the Burtons'. I just saw them," Pat said. "Don't ask me how they got there."

I ran to the phone and called Gus. He had a chip on his shoulder. "Don't blame me and the boys," he said. "We raised that fence, but a lot of the posts are rotten. Cattle can push them right over. And we don't have time to build a *new* fence."

"Well, now, Gus," I said, "they aren't my heifers, you know." I paused, struck by a useful thought. "By the way, I guess Thad's other fences aren't any too good. Gus—what if those heifers break into your place?"

An agonized bellow came through the phone. Gus had twenty head of his own feeders on pasture and he didn't want them running off their gains. "All right," he said through his teeth. "I'll work over *all* Burton's fences tomorrow. I can see I won't get a lick of work done till I do. But it'll cost something."

"I guess Thad knows that," I said. "He says good fences make good neighbors."

I didn't get a chance to tape the steers' weights for another day. It took them that long to quiet down after their romancing. Also, they were displeased with me for imprisoning them in the front pasture as far as possible from the heifers, now that the cross-fences were working again. When I did get the tape around them I was stunned. "Haven't gained *anything* this week," I told Pat. "In fact they've lost thirty pounds between them."

"Ooh, wait till I see Thad Burton," Pat said, tapping her foot. "Heifers!"

But she was not yet quite finished with heifer trouble.

The next day was Friday and she was about to take a quiet bath after lunch when she remembered that Gus was bringing us a load of straw. Not caring to be in the buff when it arrived, she phoned.

"Don't tell me they're in *again*," Gus yelled when he heard her voice, but she explained she was calling about straw, not heifers, and just wondered when—

"I'll send the boys right down with it," Gus said in the tone of an overworked man who had to do a thing right away or not at all. "Oh, and I'm going to send my shotgun with them, too."

"Sh-shotgun?" Pat said.

"Trigger's broke," Gus said, "and if Ken wouldn't mind taking it along, there's a gunsmith in town—"

"Oh, he'll be tickled to death," Pat cried. "Anything, absolutely anything."

The boys arrived shortly after with a wagonload of baled straw. They handed over the shotgun, and Pat gingerly parked it for the time being on our slanting cellar door. She didn't trust guns, broken or not. Then she ran out to the barn to oversee the hay unloading. It was just as well she hadn't taken her bath yet, for she caught a peck of loose straw on her head and down her back when she happened to stand under the loft trapdoor. As soon as the boys had gone, she tore into the house, stripped to the pink and scratched vigorously. She saw she'd have to shampoo her hair to get the straw out, so she gave up on a leisurely bath and scampered down to the basement where I had a makeshift shower.

She had progressed as far as being about to rinse off the lather, when a sound of hallooing filtered in through the curtains which formed our shower stall. She stuck her head out.

She was not expecting visitors, but it was a woman hallooing and in cultured eastern accents, rare in our parts. She squinted through her suds at the high, north cellar window looking out on our lane, and made out a sleek automobile parked there. It was full of dressy ladies.

Clattering across the basement floor, as naked as Eve except for her wooden shower clogs, she reached up and opened the window, hinged at the top, and stood on tiptoe peeking out. The ladies were strangers to her, and the car had a New York license plate. "Yes?" she said in her best formal tone, and then "*Yes*" in more of a shriek when they didn't hear her.

The ladies looked startled at this whoop from the depths. The one driving stepped out and advanced a few paces, holding her skirt up a little. "Ah . . . can you possibly tell us—just how far is it to the highway on this nice little country road, my girl?"

"Road?" Pat said. "This isn't a road. This is our pri—"

"Of course it's a road," said the lady, with the quiet authority of a club chairwoman squelching a bright idea. "Not much traveled, obviously, but a road."

For a moment my girl was tempted to let these headstrong tourists go ahead up the lane and find out for themselves that all it led to was Thad Burton's place, though years before it actually had been a county road. But then she realized what would happen. They'd have to open the gap in the fence and go all the way to Thad's house in order to find a place to turn around and come back—and she was quite sure the heifers would bolt out through the opened gap while it was going on. City folks seldom closed gaps securely even when they did it at all. A gap was just a movable twelve-foot section of a fence held by two loops of wire to a post. The loops were the latches of this crude but practical gate.

Pat shoved soapy hair out of her smarting eyes. "Now, you

listen to me, madam," she said to her visitor. "You've taken the wrong turn. Go back and follow Old Possum Road two miles north. That's the quickest way to the highway."

The lady nodded amiably. "We're in no hurry, and we like to get off the beaten path and see the countryside. And obviously this little road leads *some*where. Thank you just the same." She started back for the car, humming to herself. Pat looked frantically around for something to cover her up so she could rush out and enforce her property rights before she had the heifers again.

One of my old shirts was hanging on a nail from a joist, and a pair of my muddy jeans. She jumped into these garments, ripping hell out of one leg of the jeans when she neglected to take off her clogs first. Kicking them off entirely, she dashed barefoot to the old slanting cellar door, shoved it up, and burst out into fresh air. The lady who was driving had just begun to resume the junket up our lane, but now she stopped short and they all stared.

In her sudsy hair and the clothes five sizes too big, Pat was worth a stare, but there was something else, too. As she flung up the cellar door, Gus's shotgun which she had laid there and forgotten, sailed up, up into the breeze and came banging down. It sounded as if it was breaking in two, and she snatched it up with a howl of dismay.

The dressy visitors goggled at her for a few electric moments, and then the whole carload broke out in full-throated screams. Pat looked at them severely. Such a commotion was apt to frighten our chickens and hurt their laying. "Millicent! She's got a gun!" one lady shrieked. With a lunge, the car went backing down our lane the way it had come from, in a snaky and lurching fashion.

"Eek," Pat said, suddenly realizing that she was indeed holding a gun. Extending it at arm's length, she averted her face and fled back to the basement.

When Thad Burton came out to his farm the next day, his enthusiasm for cattle was greatly weakened, and when he saw Gus Brinkmeyer's bill for the fencing, it nearly expired. The bill came to seventy-five dollars, including some new wire and posts. Thad's first thought was to sell the heifers as fast as he could, but Gus, who had cooled down, told him he might as well keep them now that he had the fencing to hold them. Gus also offered to accept one of the heifers in full payment for the bill. One he could use, and he had taken a fancy to the thriftiest while he was working on the fence.

Gus was a goodhearted fellow when he had the time, and he also loaned Thad a scrub bull he had around, to keep the remaining heifers company for the rest of the summer. In due course they were bred, and they quieted down into gossipy matrons, and Thad got some calves out of the deal.

What we got out of it was all negative, unless you counted Pat's satisfaction over her encounter with the tourists. She considered it a moral victory and she confiscated my ripped jeans and shirt in case she needed them again for such an emergency. She declined my offer to buy her an old unloaded shotgun to add realism. She thought a slingshot would do as well, and might even be more convincing.

13

MARX, A SELF-MADE CAT

THE SMALLEST DOMESTIC ANIMAL WE EVER HAD on our farm was a barn cat, but he was better than all the cattle put together at disgracing himself. He frequently managed to make it look as if it was all our fault and he an innocent victim.

He was the survivor of a trio of black kittens given us to keep down rats in the barn. They came already named—Hart, Schaffner, and Marx—and at a glance they were identical. The difference lay in their social attitudes. The first two were so satisfied to be barn cats that they overdid it and quickly met their doom by going sound asleep in spots where cows were settling for the night. Marx, even as a kitten, did not sleep with cows. After trying for a nest in the chicken house, he settled temporarily for the hayloft. The chickens loathed cats, but he would not have been content to stay with them long even if they had not chased him. He planned to become the house cat.

Having failed with the chickens, he detoured them and soon began sneaking into the garden, which adjoined our side yard. He was still young, not much heavier than a soupbone, and had no trouble squirming through the woven-wire fence. He would then advance in an underslung fashion between rows of snap beans, aiming for our back porch. Sometimes he made it, but our dog, a Doberman pinscher named Kyrie, had standing orders to run him back to the barn whenever she saw him, so he could attend to business. He took it with good grace and kept on trying.

Soon after, he gained garden privileges by a lucky chance. While waiting under a zucchini squash plant one noontime, watching for a good chance to rush the back door, he caught a mole. As far as we knew, he had never caught anything before. "But if he'll keep the moles down," Pat said, "he's perfectly welcome to be in the garden." We moved the off-limits mark to the yard boundary and so advised Kyrie, who took it poorly. She was a rotten moler and sensitive about it.

She set up a grim watch where yard and garden met, confident that Marx would crowd his luck. Instead, he shifted strategy. He kept to the garden, but the next time we set out for an inspection tour of our forty acres of pasture and woods, he joined the party. We had not thought that cats cared for long walks, but Marx was a hiking fool. He made fewer side trips than did Kyrie, but now and then he climbed a tree for variety. On the first few jaunts he had to be carried back, exhausted. He seemed pleased by this attention, and Kyrie nearly died of jealousy. She had never been offered a lift.

Had it not been for a bed of catnip in the garden, Marx would possibly have soon made another try for the house. He rediscovered the catnip, which he and the other kittens had illegally played in soon after their arrival, and the reunion was spectacular. He fell upon the little patch, planted close to the yard, with gibbers of pleasure. He nibbled it and rolled in it, and Kyrie watched with disdain, for she was a saving type and had already put aside a small fortune in buried bones. The cat was pure wastrel. In a few days he had consumed the catnip down to bare earth and was hopefully digging up the roots.

While he was so engaged Pat came scurrying up the basement steps one day shrieking "Mouse." She had come across one in a box of rags and she believed that every mouse lived for the chance to run up inside a leg of her jeans. She took a bath to quiet her nerves, and that evening I promoted Marx to the basement to spend the night mousing.

"Do you suppose he knows what to do?" Pat asked me as we went to bed.

I said I thought they were born knowing. As a matter of fact, Marx had seemed mystified. I didn't know how one told a cat there were mice to be caught. "Sic 'em," I had said, and he had regarded me with his round yellow eyes, and meowed. He always answered, a habit we appreciated.

We went to sleep and woke up again in almost no time. "What was that?" Pat cried. A shallow metallic clatter had come from the basement. In the living room Kyrie leaped out of her wicker basket and roared. I got out of bed and went to the basement. Marx evidently had jumped up on my workbench and had knocked off a few empty coffee cans I was saving. I could see his eyes, about twice normal size, peeking around a corner of the furnace. I looked to see if a mouse was dangling from his jaws but there was none.

"Hurry up and catch it, there's a good kitty," I said, and he meowed faintly. It struck me that he sounded scared, but I preferred to think he was stalking. I returned upstairs and told Pat he had the mouse on the defensive.

We had nearly gone to sleep again when from below came a desperate wail. It was a tone Marx had never used before. "Maybe it's the mousing cry," Pat whispered. There was another wail, somewhat closer. I turned on the bedside lamp, and Kyrie, who was getting sick and tired of having her rest broken, marched to the bedroom doorway and frowned in.

I got up and opened the basement door. Marx met me on the landing with another yowl. He was quivering as I picked him up and was terribly relieved when I took him to the kitchen door and dumped him outside in disgrace. "Scared silly," I told Pat. "He'll never make a mouser."

This was only half right. Marx became a good hunter but he stayed scared of the basement and avoided it even in the daytime thereafter. Still, his flop at mousing down there did him no harm with Pat and was actually another step up the social ladder for him. This was because the basement mouse, evidently thinking the cat had come to stay, left the basement. Pat was so pleased that she allowed Marx freedom of the house grounds, lowering herself dramatically in Kyrie's esteem. Now and then she even asked him into the kitchen for a saucer of milk, mainly so she could point out to Kyrie how daintily he lapped. Kyrie went at a bowl of milk like an egg beater, but Marx's manners were so impeccable that it led to his next social triumph. He was invited to attend a little party we were giving for my brother Ted and his family.

Ted was now a doctor, in practice in St. Louis following field-hospital service in Europe with the Army during the war. He had been married a few years and had two charming and nimble-minded little girls. They were Sandra, five, and Jane, three, and Pat gave a good deal of the credit to Ted's wife Dorothy, who knew her business and had a sense of humor. They were driving out from town to have Sunday dinner with us, and in midmorning Pat glanced out the window with a chirp of dismay. "It's begun to rain," she cried. "The children will be cooped up inside all afternoon."

I was less concerned. When Ted came to the farm, he relaxed like a wet shirt, and if we were outside I needed my running shoes to keep the children from tumbling into the pond or getting butted by calves.

"We'll have to think up some indoor entertainment," Pat said. "Start thinking."

"Can't expect any help from Kyrie," I said. Our dog thought all children were pests. She didn't actually bite them but she seemed to wish afterwards that she had. To her disgust, Sandy and Jane had taken to calling her Cousin Kyrie,

at their father's urging. "The children love chickens, though,"
I said. "Shall I entice a couple of hens in for the afternoon?"

She shook her head rapidly. "Chickens aren't house-
broken."

"I suppose Marx is," I said idly. "But he's skittish around
strangers—"

"Marx! That's perfect," she said. "He's so well-mannered.
I don't know why I didn't think of him sooner."

"Now that you've thought of him, I'll get some binder
twine. The kids can wear him out chasing it all afternoon."
I got the twine and when I returned Pat was studying the
situation again.

"If only he hadn't used up all that catnip," she said. "Do
you suppose it's sprouted again?" I shook my head. It wouldn't
ever sprout again. "Say," she said. "You know what? You can
buy a catnip mouse at a drugstore."

"I don't have time. They'll be here in less than an hour."

She raced for the telephone. "Maybe I can catch them before they leave. Ted can buy one on their way out."

She let the telephone ring ten times, the way the telephone
company advised. Ted caught it on the tenth ring, sounding
so agitated that I could hear his rich baritone clear across
the room as Pat held the receiver away from her ear. "Don't
yell so," she said. "No, it isn't an emergency—it's me. I want
you to get me something at a drugstore, Ted."

"Drugstore," said Ted. "You sick? What's the matter with
you?"

"Nothing's the matter with me," Pat said, twitching her
shoulders. "If I were sick I'd call a doctor." Ted grunted. "I
want you to get me a catnip mouse at the drugstore," she
said.

There was a short silence. "What did you say, Pat?" Ted
asked in a strained voice. She repeated her order and listened for a few moments, making faces at the telephone.

"Well, what if those drugstores *do* fill your prescriptions?" she cried. "Is it a disgrace, buying a catnip mouse?"

"I'll look like a fool," Ted bawled, coming through like a public-address system.

"I haven't any more time to argue," Pat said. "I've got dinner on the stove. And if you expect any, you'd better bring that mouse, Teddy."

They arrived half an hour behind time, in the pouring rain. While Pat hugged his children, Ted, looking damp, produced a small package labeled: CATNIP MOUSE—Kitty will LOVE it. He thrust it at Pat. "Had to try five drugstores. I sounded like a catnip quack. What in hell you want it for?"

"Probably for a cat, I told him," Dotty said, "but you know Ted. Says he's never seen a cat here."

He still couldn't, for the time being. I had Marx under an apple box on the porch. He usually took to the woods when company came. We postponed his entrance until after we had eaten and then let the girls feed him to convince him he was among friends. Their father was less taken with Marx than they were.

"Where'd you get this alley cat?" he asked Pat. "Did you delouse it?"

"He's a nice clean barn cat," she said, "and better mannered than some people I could name."

"A tom, too," Ted said. "All toms are bums."

"He has the loveliest behavior of any cat I ever saw," Pat said coldly. "I hope you don't think I'd expose Sandy and Janie to anything but a nice gentlemanly cat."

When Marx had got enough petting from the girls to last him a couple of years, Pat brought out the lengths of twine and he chased them very nicely. She smiled across the room at me. Entertaining children indoors at the farm had always been hard. At last, we felt, we had the secret. From now on

Marx could be the bona fide house cat he wished to be. We could always get a barn cat.

The twine chasing lasted until Marx happened to land on top of Kyrie while aiming for a string drawn past her basket. She rose with a yelp that curled our hair and walked off stiff-legged to the porch. It was just as well. She would have been scandalized by the final act of Marx's playlet.

"Now for the surprise," Pat said. She retired the twine from service and unboxed the catnip mouse. "Kitties are ver-r-y fond of catnip, girls," she told our nieces, who were looking skeptically at the mouse as she dangled it by the tail. It looked more like a fat untidy tea bag. However, Marx's nose had begun twitching and he spoke up, sounding interested.

Sandy held out her hand. "May I feel it, Aunt Pat?" she asked, and her little sister shot out a chubby hand, too, but the catnip mouse never arrived. Marx rose to his hind legs and snatched it from Pat's hand with a lightning flick of his left front paw. It was the first time I had realized he was left-handed.

The mouse thumped sluggishly to the rug, and Marx pounced. With another swoop of paw he made a mashie shot across the room. He bounded after the mouse and for a while batted it back and forth. Now and then he inhaled deeply of it or rolled lazily on his back, inviting it to escape and then whirling and falling on it.

The children were delighted, and even Ted was mollified. "Now I see why you were such a pain about it," he told Pat. Dotty looked thoughtful. "A cat certainly has its points," she murmured. "I wonder if we could borrow one somewhere for the children on rainy days. Then I might get something done—"

She let the sentence dangle and looked harder at Marx. He had taken to throwing the catnip mouse high into the air and making one-paw catches while waltzing around on his hind legs. Then he bobbled a catch, and the mouse rolled under the sofa. He peered under after it, muttering and clawing the rug.

This was the moment to ring down the curtain, shoo Marx, and get out the dominoes, but neither Pat nor I knew it. We decided afterwards that dried catnip must be higher proof than fresh. I got a yardstick and raked the catnip mouse out from beneath the sofa. Marx grabbed it with a growl, took it under a footstool for a good chewing over, and then after an abrupt hysterical roll around the floor he seized it in his fangs and rushed out of the room.

The children were right on his trail and they all made a few roundings inside the house. Ted rubbed his jaw, and Dotty shifted her eyes to Pat, who tried a tinkly laugh. "Isn't Marx a riot?" she said. "Now, you'd simply never get Kyrie to play with—children like—this . . ." She trailed off. Marx, on his fourth or fifth trip through the house, seemed to be staggering. As the children came hallooing after him, he abruptly sat down, the mouse hanging limply from his jaws. His eyes seemed vacant. He let the mouse drop and then slowly slumped down on top of it in a stewed-rhubarb manner.

"Don't he wanna play any more?" little Janie asked.

"What's the matter with him, Uncle Ken?" Sandy said.

I hesitated, but Ted had no blocks about telling his children the seamy facts. "He's on a bust, kids," he said. "Ho, ho, he's drunk as a skunk on Aunt Pat's catnip." He hugged

himself. "Thanks for the show, Pat," he said, and guffawed.

"He is not," she cried. "Anyway, it isn't the same thing at all, Teddy." She glanced uneasily at the children, who were poking our blotto cat to no effect. "He's . . . just tired, honey," she said to Sandy.

Ted's elder daughter gave Marx a professional glance. "He's drunk," she said briefly.

"Dwunk," said Janie. "Dwunk as a skunk."

Marx came to his senses temporarily while Dotty was washing the children's hands, and tottered behind the sofa where he promptly went fast asleep again. I banished him outside as soon as our company had left and the children could not witness his disgraceful weaving gait across the yard.

We did not even see him again for two days, and then he was a sight. For a cat with social ambitions he had picked the worst possible place to sleep off his catnip jag—a pile of fresh horse manure we had had delivered for compost purposes. It had damaged his coat, and patches came off when he set to licking himself respectable. He looked as if moths had got to him and he was not allowed in the house again until fall, and then only for a compelling romantic reason.

The reason was another party, a Halloween party. It was not our party, but my wife became involved because her help was sought by a young neighbor girl who was trying to assemble a prize-winning costume. She was Bessie Brinkmeyer, a rather coltish sixteen-year-old niece of Daisy and Gus Brinkmeyer's. Since there isn't much leeway in the choice of costumes at a Halloween party, Bessie thought she might as well go as a witch and be done with it. Pat agreed to help on one condition: Bessie should go as a *pretty* witch.

"Bessie's getting to be an attractive child," Pat told me, "but nobody's noticed it yet, including her. She has good bone structure and lovely hair, and if I can help fix her up so people will notice her, it'll do wonders for her personality."

Between Pat and Daisy, Bessie got fixed up with a flary black taffeta skirt, paper witch hat, and a frilly blouse. When she came by on the afternoon before the party that night, Pat added an eye mask and a neck ribbon of black velvet with a spray of tiny yellow chrysanthemums on it. That did it, she felt, but the glamorous new Bessie had become a perfectionist. She wanted a black cat to complete her costume. She asked to borrow Marx.

Pat retreated. Since his catnip brawl she was not so sure of Marx. She suggested a broom instead, but Bessie pleaded so for Marx that Pat called him in for a fitting.

His coat had grown out again and he had his poise back, but he stopped short at Bessie in her witch outfit and would have left. However, she spoke, and he recognized her voice. He sat down and stared at her.

"An eight-pound cat is a load to carry around all evening," Pat pointed out. "A broom would be lots easier to manage, Bessie."

"Oh, he'll be no more trouble than a purse," said Bessie, rapidly draping Marx over one arm. "See? And I bet nobody else will bring a black cat. Why, he'll probably help me win first prize." It was a remark that Pat remembered with great clarity. "I'll pick him up after supper on the way to the party, okay?" Bessie said, which was the arrangement when I got home from work and Pat asked what I thought of it.

"Not much," I said. "Who wants to carry a cat all night?"

"He might get excited and scratch her, too."

I looked at Marx. "Too bad we haven't got another catnip mouse to drug him with."

"We've got whisky," she said. "Remember how it calmed Kyrie?" I had given our dog an ounce of bourbon in milk one night during a bad thunderstorm, and it had sent her into dreamland. I estimated that she would make about seven of Marx, which figured out to a scant teaspoon of whisky. I mixed it with milk, and he lapped it up and called for more.

"He looks just the same to me," Pat said after half an hour, "and we haven't much more time." I prepared another milk punch. "Put in a couple of spoonfuls," she said. "Let's make sure." I sighed and did so. It was bonded bourbon I was saving for some occasion, such as getting a raise. By the time Bessie arrived for him the only effect the liquor had had on Marx was to make him totally indifferent to Kyrie.

I had the impression Bessie looked surprisingly fetching but I was paying more attention to our cat. He made no resistance to leaving with her, and hanging on her arm in a loose horseshoe fashion, he seemed to wear a smile. I thought he hiccuped once on the way out.

"He's going to sleep," Pat whispered to me as Bessie bore him off to her folks' car. "It's certainly a load off my mind. And I really think Bessie has a very good chance for the costume prize."

Bessie did win first prize. But the circumstances under which she won it caused quite a bit of snippy comment in her circle afterwards, and reflected on Pat. The three male judges of the costumes (nonlocal gentlemen, to avoid any taint of favoritism) may not have realized what happened.

Marx was sound asleep over Bessie's arm when she arrived, and he stayed that way for the first part of the evening, stirring only occasionally. He was as helpful as her mask in keeping Bessie a mystery, too. Even most of those who suspected her identity under the new glamour were thrown off by knowing her folks did not own a black cat. The community at large felt it was tempting bad luck to own one.

Shortly before the costumes were to be judged, Marx began waking up. He raised his head, blinked, and tried to focus, Bessie reported later. He seemed to her mildly interested but not at all excited. Then, as the line of young folks formed up for parading before the judges on a platform,

Marx became fascinated by the costume of a girl just ahead of Bessie.

Also dressed as a Halloween witch (most of the girls were, it turned out), this one had a few modern touches to her outfit. She was wearing her little brother's pinwheel beanie cap and she had around her waist a girdle of toy balloons, apparently a replacement for the old flying broomstick. Bessie was looking at these doodads, too, and so failed to notice Marx reaching out his trusty left front paw to pat one of the balloons.

Had he been cold sober he would not, I think, have unsheathed his claws. But he did so, and the balloon exploded in his face. Its owner's back was turned, and there was enough background noise so that, though she wiggled slightly, she did not seem to notice the burst, but Marx went simply wild. Bessie clamped him to her and then tried to hold him with both her hands, and he went wilder.

Wrenching free, he plunged backwards down the length of her light skirt, his razor claws bared to the hilt. He vanished in the crowd as Bessie stared down at her skirt. It was not a very long one and now it was slashed from waist to hem. She started to run away, but the line was already moving toward the judges, and the audience was ringed all around, cutting off escape.

Bessie gripped her rent skirt with one desperate hand and hoped nobody would notice. But Pat had been right about Bessie's bone structure, especially her legs. They had been shaping up during the summer and had suddenly become one of her most striking points. And now, every time she took a step, a sensational flash of lovely calf and thigh appeared through the slash of her skirt. There was a chorus of gasps from the onlookers, and Daisy Brinkmeyer nearly died when she saw her niece's legs parading around the platform.

The judges, though, were deeply impressed. They didn't know it was an accident. They had seen plenty of movies of exotic dancers dressed like that, and Bessie looked both exotic and delightful, quite a twist on all the other haglike Halloween witches present.

She walked off with first prize, a silver-plated dresser set, and it did wonders for her morale, even though Daisy pinned the skirt right up as soon as she got her hands on Bessie and told everybody it was all the Kraft cat's fault. Practically all the women were sure Pat had secretly arranged it to help cop first prize, and treated her coolly later.

But for Marx the party was a social disaster. He had to find his way home from it in the dark by himself, and he had several fights on the way. We found him sleeping it off in the barn the next day, with a torn ear and a look of disillusionment. For a long time afterwards he showed little enthusiasm for coming near the house or even the yard, and he took to smelling all milk earnestly before he drank it.

14

KYRIE, THE DOG WHO LIKED THINGS NICE

IFE ON THE FARM SUITED KYRIE PERFECTLY, especially after we had remodeled the house during our second year there, giving her a more elegant environment. She had a litter of seven pups during the remodeling and then gave up motherhood permanently for a career as a country estate dog. So she thought.

The pastoral pattern was shattered when, after six years on the farm, we sold it. Kyrie's vocabulary—so large that we had to spell unpopular words in her hearing—did not include real estate terms, so the move that followed came as a shock, and no wonder. After having her own forty acres of hilly fields and woods and a pond full of sporty frogs, she was being demoted to a cramped house trailer, for we planned a spell of travel.

The trailer, only half the size of our farm living room, was a complete little house, needing merely water, electric, and waste lines attached when in use. It cost three thousand dollars, and though we suspected Kyrie might feel a bit cramped in it, she had always enjoyed automobile rides.

Aside from storage drawers and cabinets in the trailer's kitchen, there were three big closets and eight cupboards in other places—a temptation when we started loading up to leave. We began adding items we hadn't dreamed of taking: fifty-four jars of things from the fruit cellar; a huge pressure cooker and a big brass apple-butter kettle; two extra sets of mixing bowls and an extra electric mixer; a turkey platter and hurricane lamps; a coal shovel, two milk buckets, and some nice boards I thought might come in handy. Also all the clothes we owned, and then I saw Pat approaching with a pair of rubber boots and her favorite hoe. "Well, now," I said.

She tossed her head. "I just saw you carry in the timber saw." I removed the saw, and she gave up her boots and hoe, but at the last minute she remembered her ironing board and wouldn't leave without it. We dropped it behind the sofa in the rear room and put Kyrie's basket in the room. Our stylish dog, who at first had taken the trailer for a fancy new chicken house, had begun chewing her nails. When she saw her basket go in, she slumped in the driveway, her ears at half-mast.

I hitched up, put her in the back seat of the car, and got our freight moving. As we rolled down the farm lane for the last time, she glanced out the back window, saw that the trailer was coming with us, and flung herself down on the seat with a moan.

It had been eleven years since Pat and I had gone off on a vacation, so we planned to head for New Orleans and then make a coastal tour east and north and jog west across the country from New England. It hadn't occurred to us that there were two more votes to be counted. There was Kyrie's and there was the trailer's.

Towing a trailer was not the lark it had seemed when reading the trailer fan magazines. The car felt tail-heavy and sluggish. As we trundled down the highway the trailer began a sedate weaving. I smacked the electric-brake lever fastened to the steering column, the brakes shrieked, and the trailer gave us a tremendous yank, snapping all our heads forward. A passing truck driver swerved to the shoulder of the road, and Kyrie jumped straight up in the back seat. Pat moistened her lips.

Presently a huge interstate moving van zoomed by, creating a partial vacuum that sucked the trailer toward the center line. Both Pat and Kyrie rose out of their seats and exchanged whoops of dismay. I cut our speed to a mincing twenty miles an hour, and a line of cars honked themselves hoarse behind us until we decided to do them a favor and stop for the night. We had got a late start and thought we'd better find a nice trailer park while it was still light.

"No trailer parks around here," said the man at a filling station I pulled into, "but for a buck you can park it back of the station and hitch up to water and electric."

We did. "Don't unfasten the car," Pat said, looking around at the weeds that surrounded this shanty spot. "I might want to leave in a hurry."

She set to fixing dinner, and I took some chow back to Kyrie, installed now in her rear bedroom. "Good heavens, the dishes," I heard Pat saying in the kitchen. They and the glassware had slid in the cabinet over the sink at every swerve in the road, and the breakage was impressive.

"She's doing a doughnut," I said, returning with the untouched chow. "Sore about something."

"Don't you feel well?" Pat asked Kyrie, going back to pay a call. Kyrie looked sourly around her little room and lay down again in a tighter knot, nose to tail. We gave her up and had our own dinner off a combination table-buffet Pat was keeping four quilts in, and spent the evening exploring our other storage. I yawned and unfolded the lounge that was doubling in the living room as our bed. "Before I undress," Pat said, "would you mind stepping outside?"

"Good Lord," I said. "We've been married seventeen years."

"I want to be sure nobody can see *in.*"

I took Kyrie along for her evening run and found it impossible to see in through the metal slat blinds. "Just the same," Pat said when I reported this, "I'm glad we've got a watchdog along. I've never slept in back of a filling station in my life." She became a little less pleased with the watchdog after we had been in bed five minutes. "Listen," she said to me. "She's doing it."

"Kyrie!" I yelled, making the trailer shudder. "Stop that."

"Won't do a bit of good," Pat said. "You know how she is about audible breathing." It was a form of discipline our dog used on us. "You'll have to shut the door to her room," Pat said.

I went back, closed the sliding door, and returned to bed, feeling the way with my shins. A few minutes later, Pat shook me awake. "I just thought of something," she said. "What good is a watchdog all closed up?"

I went back and slid the door open again. Audible breathing pursued me back to bed, and I went to sleep with the pillow over my head.

The trailer bided its time until we had crossed the Tennessee line into Mississippi. Then one of its two tires went down. We were told so by a passing driver. "Hi," he said cheerily. "Y'all got one hell of a flat on that thing."

The flat was on the right-hand wheel, and I jacked it up and pulled the rim while Pat waved traffic by. There was no spare, so I unhitched the car and we drove back to a filling station with the tire, Pat joining Kyrie in chewing nails. "I might need a new tube," I told the man. "Don't know how long it was flat."

"You'll need a new tire too," he said, looking it over. "This'n got all chawed up inside. Lucky I got this size." The luck cost thirty-two dollars and both my passengers' nerves. When we were mobile again, Pat kept twisting around to look back at the trailer, and Kyrie twisted with her.

"Calm down, everybody," I said. "We probably just picked up a spike."

Pat and Kyrie exchanged looks.

"Might not happen again in twenty thousand miles," I said.

"I think we overloaded that thing," Pat said in a rush. So did I, but I had hated to say so. "Let's stop in Jackson and ship some stuff back," she said. Kyrie clicked her teeth nervously in agreement.

I had planned merely to wave pleasantly at Jackson in passing, but instead we hunted up a trailer park when we got there. "Number twenty space," said a woman in the office. "There's a nice shade tree there." We crawled over to number twenty. The tree crowded one side of the narrow slot, and another trailer jammed the other side.

"Care to back it in?" I asked the woman. "I'm not very exper—"

"I'd be scared to death," she said. "I might break something." I saw that a goodly crowd of park residents was gathering for the ceremony. They always did, I found out later, and sometimes laid bets on it if the driver seemed to be turning green in the face. Our trailer salesman had told me how to back: If you want the trailer to swing left, turn your wheels to make the car swing to the right. It sounded wrong but it was right.

"Gee," Pat said, "that was easy, wasn't it?" She and Kyrie had been watching from the sidelines. "You did it so well, I think we ought to stay here a few days."

We loaded up four suitcases with the heavier storage from the trailer, shipped them back to St. Louis, and got acquainted with Jackson. "I like it here," Pat said after the third day, "and anyway, Kyrie's too nervous to leave yet." Kyrie was behaving as if the trailer park was a pesthouse. Most of the time she spent curled in her basket, and when a little terrier sauntered over to pass the time of day, she bared her teeth and chased him back under his own trailer.

After we had been there a week, Pat ran out of excuses, and I hitched up. The old residents waved us off, and the terrier came out into the open air again. "We're leaving too soon," Pat said. "I should have done some more shopping. I'll bet Kyrie's chow is all gone."

I shook my head. "She's hardly touched it."

"I *thought* she was losing weight," Pat exclaimed. "Her stomach's going."

As we approached Columbia, Mississippi, another kindly motorist flagged us. "*Flat*," he said, jerking his thumb backward. This time it was the trailer's left-hand wheel.

"We didn't unload enough stuff," Pat cried. I felt it was faulty distribution of what remained. We bought another new tire and tube and spent the night in back of the filling station that sold them to us.

The next morning's trip was an absolute blank, scenically. We all kept expecting another tire failure, and we got it. Somewhere in Louisiana the trailer began tracking poorly. I found the right-hand tire was going soft, but by pumping air in we made it to a crossroads filling station. "The man thinks we caught it in time and the tire's not hurt," I told Pat, who had stayed in the car. "Take about an hour to vulcanize the tube." Kyrie was listening in the back seat, working on her nails again.

"Let's leave that damn trailer here and drive on to New Orleans," Pat said suddenly. "We can send one of those professional towers back for it."

I stared into the window, and she and Kyrie stared right back. "We want to enjoy New Orleans," she said, "not arrive nervous wrecks."

I squared it with the filling-station man and unhitched the car, and as we left the trailer standing forlornly behind us on one wheel and a jack, I thought of something. We hadn't given the trailer a name. Whenever we'd bought a car we had usually given it a name because it was handy to have one if only to cuss it out with. It seemed an odd omission in the case of the trailer, and I was afraid that any name we might pick now would be unprintable.

"What's the first one on your list?" I asked Pat as we set out for dinner after checking into a motel on Gentilly Road. For months she had been babbling about the New Orleans restaurants.

"I'll decide on the way downtown," she murmured. "I hope Kyrie won't be nervous in that motel room by herself." I had been studying a map of the city and had memorized one sure route to the French Quarter. I didn't want to memorize two and get lost. Pat, who usually said "down" when she meant "up," or "up" when she meant "over," hadn't looked at the map. She understood that there were more than restaurants in the French Quarter, and she didn't intend to wander around without me. "Here's a place," she said before we had gone a block.

It was not a gourmet setup. In fact it was kind of a joint. "That's on your list?" I cried.

"No," she said, "but I'm not dressed up enough to go downtown, and I'm tired, and I don't think we ought to leave Kyrie alone so long after the trip she's had." We had hamburgers, and so back to bed.

Next day we looked up a trailer park, and for twenty-five dollars the owner went after our trailer and dragged it back. He had no tire trouble with it and said it wasn't overloaded. Everybody in the trailer park had a different theory on the cause of our troubles, so I yanked off the trailer's tires and looked up a tire expert downtown. It was no mystery to him. "You're slicing up tubes like baloney," he said. "You need flaps—liners between tubes and rims." We had them installed, and I put the trailer's flapped tires back on.

Pat and Kyrie watched me narrowly, and Pat finally spoke

for both: "If it needs those things, why didn't the factory put them on?"

I didn't know, but I fired a letter back to the dealer, advising him he owed us $127.56—our total out-of-pocket for tires, tubes, flaps, meals, motel rent and other emergency expenses, including a flashlight Pat had bought to blind passing traffic in case we were stranded on a roadside after dark. The dealer ruffled up and squawked at the miscellaneous bits, but bravely admitted the factory was at fault in forgetting flaps. It took two weeks of correspondence to collect the eighty dollars we compromised on, and I then announced we were ready to push on.

"There's lots more to see here," Pat said. "We haven't been to all the restaurants, and Kyrie needs more exercise in the park."

"Come on," I said. "Other places have restaurants and parks." Kyrie went into her doughnut and breathed at me.

"And there's Mardi Gras," Pat said.

"That was all over before we got here."

"There's another one coming. Next year."

"Next year!" I began making things secure for travel. "By then we'll have about six thousand more miles behind us." It was an estimate I missed by a couple of zeros.

We headed east toward Mississippi's gulf coast along Highway 90, Pat wearing ruts in the floor boards and Kyrie sitting like an iron deer in the back seat. "Remember—we're going to visit the MacDougals in Long Beach," Pat said. They were friends who ran a motel, but since they had no trailer accommodations we looked up a place near by to lay over for a night when we got in the vicinity. It was a new park, just opened, and we were the first customers. The owner, a Mr. Goldberg, almost hugged us and didn't object to Kyrie. He had a Doberman of his own, tearing around his yard, a sight that sent Kyrie into another fit of melancholia.

Mr. Goldberg skipped ahead to show me where to put the trailer. The park was the rear of his big lot, and none too roomy. "You can park it," I said, scrambling out.

"I'll guide you," he said, locking his arms behind his back.

I got back in and geed and hawed and chewed up his clam-shell drive for ten minutes, and we finished by hand, he and I lifting the hitch together and grunting the trailer into place. We hung onto each other, blowing. "N-nothing to it," he gasped. "A cinch," I said between wheezes, patting the trailer. "She's solid as a rock."

It was a prophetic remark. The trailer, though I didn't dream it yet, was there to stay.

"Why do you want to go traipsing all over the country," asked our friend MacDougal, "when you're already in the best part of it?" We were sitting in the living room of their house at the motel, with Mac carrying on his end of the con-versation in between hopping in and out to take care of cus-tomers. It made it hard to argue with him. He was gone while I was answering one blast, and back just in time to throw an-other.

Pat wasn't arguing. "I like it here," she kept saying.

"You owe it to yourselves to look around, at least," said Mac, popping in for another commercial.

"Mac loves the bayou country," said his wife as he sprang out the door again to get somebody clean towels.

"Good fishing there, too," he yelled back from the porch.

"It won't hurt to look," Pat said.

So we looked.

"Have you got something on about forty acres on a bayou?" I asked the first real estate man we talked to, in Gulfport. Since our farm had been that size, we thought it was about right. The salesman steadied himself on the edge of his desk.

"Fo—*rty* acres?" he said in a sliding trombone voice.

"We don't mind if it's bigger," I said, "if the place is mostly woods."

"On a bayou?" he said weakly.

"Something secluded, please," I said.

He fanned himself with an earnest-money receipt. "Would you consider something just a little smaller?"

"How much smaller?" Pat asked.

"Well-l-l," he said. "It's very secluded. Be glad to show you."

We went, in our car because Pat didn't want Kyrie, enthroned on the back seat, to worry while we were gone. The paved road ended after a few miles, and we mushed on along a sandy lane through woods. "I hope we don't get stuck," Pat said. "This place certainly *must* be secluded."

"Oh, very," said the salesman. "Here it is right now."

I stopped the car. We were in a clearing, where the lane ended. A small cottage was ahead. Beside it, thirty feet away, was another. Beside that was another. Beside that one was another. . . .

"And the bayou's right over—" the salesman began.

"*Secluded,*" Pat cried, finding her tongue.

"Yes, ma'am," said the salesman, getting out. "Six miles from town if it's an inch. Every place here has a good sixty-front-footage on the bayou, too."

Pat also got out of the car, opened the back door, and got right back in. "I'll sit with Kyrie on the way back," she said coldly.

"Don't you want to see the place, ma'am?" the salesman asked, gaping.

"No," she said. "Secluded!" Kyrie muttered and went into her doughnut. At that, she was the most cheerful member of the party on the return trip.

We tried other real estate offices in Gulfport and elsewhere, with no better luck. Some had no bayou frontage listed at all, and it began to dawn on us that it was scarce. We stopped talking about forty acres even before we had worked our way through all the salesmen, to save them from strokes.

"Well, that does it," I said when we had drawn our twentieth or so blank. "Let's hitch up and continue our trip."

"Let's try Pass Christian once more," Pat said. The towns were strung out along the coast like a daisy chain, and in Pass Christian there was one real estate office we hadn't tried. They had been out to lunch when we were there.

We went back, and they were in, Mr. Thong and his son Bert. Mr. Thong looked to be an old hand at the business. He had a headful of stand-up white hair and an air of not caring if he sold anything so long as he got in a lot of good visiting.

"Bayou prop'ty, hm-m," he said, idly thumbing a listings notebook. "By the way, you folks tried the stuffed flounder since you've been here? Had a mighty fine one for lunch—"

"How about the Danton place, Pop?" Bert said into his ear. "On Arcadia Bayou."

"So 'tis," said Mr. Thong. "You folks from Missouri, you say? Had a cousin once—"

"How about Walker's place, Pop?" Bert cried. "Bayou Portage."

"Portage," said Mr. Thong. "Nice neighborhood. Cousin was in St. Joe. Or was it St. Louis—?"

"How about Cassidy's place on Johnson Bayou, Pop?" Bert yelled. His father was a little hard of hearing, we began to realize.

"Well, you take the folks along, boy," Mr. Thong said, giving up. "Might run on something or other they take a fancy to."

We went in Bert's car, Pat having decided Kyrie wouldn't get lonesome parked in Pass Christian, which had a nice small-town flavor, and set out to see the three places Bert had roared out to his father. Aside from that, Bert was soft-sell and a cheery companion.

"This is pretty run-down," Pat said of the Cassidy place, a

shotgun type of frame house overlooking a marshy bayou area.

"Not much to it," Bert agreed. "Might do something with it, though. Low enough price." The price was $6,500.

When we got to the Danton property, I was not impressed, though it was on higher ground and the bayou was attractive. "I think the roof leaks," I said, gazing at an enormous stain on the ceiling of one room.

"Looks that way, sure enough," Bert said. "I'd better tell Mr. Danton to fix it. Might as well have the termite man check it, too. Not a bad price, though." The price here was $11,000, but the house was one of those that defied remodeling.

Pat gave Bert a baffled look, and we went on to the Walker place. It was a frame house built up from the ground on piers, as were most older places. The gallery—porch to us—was L-shaped, with one end enclosed as a makeshift kitchen. "Never mind the termites and roof," Pat said, hurrying toward the wooden porch steps. "Let's just look—eek!" One tread of the steps was giving way under her.

"Dry rot," Bert said. "Have to rebuild wood steps every three years."

We walked down to look at the bayou. "Ooh, I like this," Pat said. "It's more like a river." It was about 50 feet wide and looped around the 120-foot frontage of the property, which was some 600 feet long. A channel had been cut in from one side to form a little harbor where a shabby skiff floated, half full of water. "Does the skiff come with it?" Pat asked.

Bert shrugged. "Don't see why anybody'd haul the thing off," he said, and leaped into the air. "Snake, snake," he yelled happily, and something slithered into the palmetto clumps. We all galloped back up the slope to the house, tried another flight of steps not quite so rotten, and looked the place over. It had three bedrooms, living room, and bathroom, not counting the so-so kitchen. The owner, who used it as a week-end place, was asking $10,000, Bert said, and thought it worth twelve.

We all went back to the real estate office. "Lady almost fell through Walker's steps, Pop," Bert said cheerfully.

"Boy," his father said, looking at him over his glasses, "that's when you're supposed to be telling prospects all about the flowers and trees and things, so's they don't notice."

"I'm afraid we'd have to spend too much money on the place," I said.

"Some do, some don't," said Mr. Thong. "You could make an offer."

We rejoined Kyrie and returned to our trailer, to her great gloom. Apparently she thought we had bought her a farm, we were gone so long.

We went back by ourselves the next day and prowled around. Kyrie, who hadn't had a chance to run and jump without a leash since we had left the farm, acted as if she had found paradise.

"This place has possibilities," Pat said, "for remodeling."

"Expensive ones," I said. "And do you call this seclusion?" There were houses on each side, one of them practically on top of the common property line. I pointed to it.

"Well," Pat said, "I guess we just have to accept the fact—" She looked harder. "Oh, hello." The neighbor man and his wife, I saw, were smiling at us through a bamboo clump on the fence line, and Kyrie was fawning on them.

"We're the Feinsteins," said the man. "You're buying the Walker place, I hope?"

"We'd love to have permanent neighbors," Mrs. Feinstein said, fondling Kyrie. "We love your dog."

"We may make an offer," Pat murmured, edging away from me.

"Let's take a run down the bayou," Mr. Feinstein cried. "We've got an outboard."

Mr. Feinstein was retired, but after the bayou ride I was not surprised to learn he had been a salesman all his life. The bayou wound its way down to Bay St. Louis like a delightful little jungle river, with fish leaping about the skiff, and Mr. Feinstein sat back and let it do the selling. A few days later we arranged to buy the Walker place for $8,500, after a trial balloon of $5,000, based on the probable expense of remodeling, had nearly given Walker apoplexy by long-distance telephone.

"But the trailer's practically new," Pat said to me, "and worth every penny of three thousand dollars, so we'll get that back." We had been told that good used trailers were hard to find. Our trailer salesman in St. Louis had told us. They hadn't heard about it in Mississippi.

The best offer we got was that we leave the trailer with a dealer on consignment, for a 10 per cent commission if sold. Unfortunately, too, we had paid cash for the trailer, and everybody wanted financing. With a new trailer, financing came automatically, like a hang-over after a party.

We went moping back to our drug on the market, which now had some company in the trailer park, to Mr. Goldberg's joy. "It hasn't got so much as a scratch on it," Pat said.

I nodded. "It's a better trailer than it was four weeks ago when it was brand-new and without flaps."

"It's efficient and handy and perfectly lovely," she said, "and Kyrie and I are sick and tired of living in it."

"Have to stay till we sell it. We'll run an ad."

We put an ad in the *Gulfport Herald* and met some interesting people who had always wanted to inspect a trailer. Pat and Kyrie grew more restive, and Pat said that living in a trailer was breaking Kyrie's spirit, especially now that the park was filling up. "It's not doing my spirit any good either," she said. "Let's move to our bayou house. Mr. Goldberg can show the trailer to anybody who might answer the ad."

We had got well acquainted with Mr. Goldberg during the

first few days when we were his only chicks, and I had formed a great respect for his business sense. "Maybe he could sell this white elephant for us," I said. I looked him up in the washroom, where he was tinkering with the automatic washer.

"What do you want for the trailer?" he asked. I told him we had paid $3,000, getting a little off for cash, and it was still like new.

He rubbed his ear. "Cash, nobody's got," he said. "Except, maybe, for a big bargain."

I took a hitch in my belt. "Twenty-five hundred?"

"Twenty-four ninety-five. For that, you could sell it yourself."

"I've tried," I said. "You sell it and we'll make the commission three hundred dollars."

"I'll draw up a contract," Mr. Goldberg said. He did, in five minutes, and we signed it in the trailer. "You'll have to put a regular bed in here," he said, making a fast survey. "I can get one at a good price." He left, waving the contract signatures dry.

"Do you think he can sell it?" Pat asked me as we got things together to move.

"If he can't, we'll have to attach it to the bayou house," I said, "because that'll be the only remodeling we can afford."

The bayou house had enough odds and ends of furniture for us to get along on for a while and an ancient electric stove that clicked and swore whenever we switched it on. Kyrie seemed to think the house much too bare for her position in society but she cheered up when she realized the trailer had passed out of her life forever. She set to cultivating the Feinsteins, and I fell to work with Mr. Feinstein's toolbox on the skiff. It needed new seats, new bracing, new floor slats, recaulking, and paint. It looked quite spruce when done, and we christened it *Sandyjane*, for our nieces, but it was the only

remodeling we did, for the time being. The only change we
made in the house was to have a telephone installed, and
even that seemed a waste of money for the first two weeks.
But then it rang and friend Goldberg was on the other end.

"Any luck yet?" I said.

"Well, I had to buy a table, too," he said. "With the bed,
it's fifty dollars. They insisted."

"Who insisted?"

"Why, the customers," he said.

I caught my breath. "You *sold* it?"

"Sure," he said. "Cash money."

"Goldie," I said, "tell me something. How in hell did you
find a customer?"

"I just asked myself: 'Goldberg, where do you find people
who need a trailer?' and I went there and found them."

"Went where?"

"To a place where they sell trailers, what else?" he said.
"Pretty soon this young couple comes along asking the salesman how much off for cash. At most a hundred dollars, he
tells them. So they leave, naturally, and I follow their car. 'I
can save you *five* hundred,' I tell them when I catch up. 'Follow me.' So they do, and they save five hundred dollars. They

love your trailer, and I gave them one month free park rent. That's for good will."

Our check came to $2,145. "Well, we *had* to sell the thing," Pat said. "I honestly don't think Kyrie could have stood it much longer, and of all the dogs we've had, she's the most—"

"Expensive," I said. I did a little figuring. "Counting her original purchase price, plus the loss on the trailer, she has now cost us $915 aside from upkeep." I glanced around. "And where is the spendthrift, by the way, now that we have provided her with her own waterfront estate?"

"Visiting the Feinsteins," Pat said. "She does like gracious surroundings."

15

FUSS AND FEATHERS

EFORE WE WENT TO MISSISSIPPI, PAT AND I HAD been the practical type of bird watchers on our Missouri farm. The birds we watched were mostly chickens, and we watched them to see if they were laying. We had nothing against the more usual type of bird watching. It was merely that we had no time to think about it.

When we settled down on Bayou Portage we still had no time for the birds for a while. After the trailer was sold, we started remodeling the house, and it was summertime. We had thought that Missouri was hot in the summer. Mississippi was terrific. After the carpenters, plumbers, electricians, and painters finally finished and left us alone in our spruced-up house, we were too whipped for a while to do anything but sprawl in lounge chairs on the gallery, mopping perspiration and looking weakly up into the leafy pecan trees that surrounded the house. Green, we understood, was a restful color.

It was while we were doing this that we noticed the mockingbird. It was studying us, craning its neck and occasionally uttering cries that sounded like "Hop to it!" Every house had its own mockingbird, we found out later. They bossed the other nonpredatory birds except the pileated woodpecker, which was the size of a flying pot roast, and the tiny hummingbirds, which were too fast and quick-tempered to meddle with. The mockingbirds were also severe with people, and

when out of sorts would light near the house and practice
their rusty-hinge and dry-bearing selections. This was greatly
admired.

"Lookit the bird," Pat murmured from her lounge on the
gallery. "I wonder what it is?"

My recognition was limited to Leghorns, Plymouth rocks,
and the like.

"There's another," Pat said as a chickadee zipped by. "Little bitty one." A hairy woodpecker dropped in to inspect the
pecan tree trunk, and Pat sat up. "Say—there are all *kinds* of
birds around here," she said. "We'd better get a bird book."

We drove to Pass Christian, about two miles from our
place, and looked up the library. Jeanne Knost, the helpful
librarian, instantly identified the mockingbird from Pat's de-
scription and forgave her not knowing it. She loaned us the
bird books she had, and my wife became an expert in two
or three days when she spotted a crested flycatcher and a
hooded warbler, and was able to pursue her research with an
air of authority at the larger Harrison County library in Gulfport. There, librarian Maria Person, deceived by my Joanie-
come-lately, rushed around and fetched up every last bird
guide in the place, quite a stack. Pat pored through them at
home and then sent off and bought the biggest one.

During this period I was not idle. "I've been noticing," Pat
had said, "that everybody around here has bird feeders."

"I guess you can buy them," I said. "Maybe the Feinsteins
will pick one up for us in New Orleans next time they go."
Our neighbors were very nice about doing such errands, as
well as lending us anything they owned and leaving the key
to their house with us when they were away, in case we
thought of something else to borrow.

"You can easily make a bird feeder," Pat said. "You've got
all that scrap lumber left over from the remodeling."

I had quite a bit of it in the garage we had built. I occasionally fell over it at night so I was willing to trim the pile down. First I used some of it to build a couple of sawhorses to work on, while Pat kept asking when I was going to get started. I then built a bird feeder out of two squares of plywood and a piece of four-by-four, a sort of squatty pedestal table.

"Gee, there was nothing to that, was there?" Pat said. "And you've got lots of stuff left."

I took the hint and built another. She put bread crumbs on them and in no time we had a sudden population of blue jays gabbling happily around the feeder tables, wing to wing, a couple of dozen.

"We need more feeders," Pat said presently. "No other bird has a chance with all these jays." The mockingbird did but he was indifferent to bread crumbs after one taste and let the jays alone. Kyrie would have been glad to run the jays off and eat the bread crumbs herself, but Pat forbade it. Our dog was nonselective, regarding all birds as unnecessary.

I was tired of making pedestal feeders, so I ran off some other designs—tall tripod things, tier-table jobs, and one to hang from a tree limb. It merely whetted Pat's appetite for them. She was experimenting with suet and corn flakes, and had discovered that the mockingbird would accept blanched almonds. I was willing to accept almonds myself, so in self-defense I looked up a cheaper treat after a time and this led to difficulties. But shortly before it happened we discovered something that charmed my wife: Bird watching/feeding was a brisk social asset. We were enlightened by the neighbors on our other side.

They were the Gentrys, retired. We were only a little older than their eldest child, so Mrs. Gentry took a kindly see-here-my-dear attitude toward Pat at once. Mr. Gentry and I were more formal and were still making little bows to each other through the ligustrum hedge some time after Pat and Mrs.

Gentry were trading recipes and azalea cuttings. The Gentrys were famous bird watchers and had several feeders on a brick terrace where they and their friends could see the birds from the front gallery.

While soaking up her bird lore, Pat happened to run next door to take Mrs. Gentry a pie she had just baked, and found her peeking at a new arrival on the terrace. Pat peeked too. "Rose-breasted grosbeak," she said at once, luckily remembering the picture in her bird book. Mrs. Gentry stared at her.

"You never told me you knew the birds," she said crossly.

"Oh, I just know a few," said Pat. This was strictly true. She knew only a few as yet. However, it sounded sweetly modest. Mrs. Gentry approved of this and then revealed that bird watching was a violent passion with the pillars of Dixie society and even jostled for precedence with knowing who was related to General Lee. Though Pat had no more social ambitions than a 'possum, this seemed to please her.

Not long after this episode Mrs. Gentry strolled over and caught me turning out bird feeders like a Detroit assembly line. We already had eight or ten of them set up and in use in scattered spots, and when Mrs. Gentry saw what was going forward on the sawhorses she grew a bit tart.

"Well, no wonder we aren't getting as many birds at our place as usual," she said. "They're all coming here. How many feeders do you plan to put out, for mercy sakes?"

Pat ducked the question and said something about experimenting with various kinds till we saw which was best. Actually, she had no intention of discarding any of them. The only experimenting she was doing was with what she put on the feeders. She was featuring cooked oatmeal that week, larded with raisins, and also had had great success with a crawfish, which was carried off by a dumfounded red-bellied woodpecker.

The Feinsteins had no pangs over our growing number of feeders. Though they, too, fed the birds, they were so glad we had moved next door that they waived our competition. One big reason they were glad for permanent neighbors was so there would be somebody to chase a certain mule out of their yard when they were away. They went to New Orleans frequently, and the mule, known to us as The Brain, had learned to open their gate. He could open ours, too, and though the Gentrys had installed a latch that baffled him after he had once got in and pruned their gardenias to the ground, it was one of the very few gates that kept him out. Like any other livestock in that section of Mississippi, the mule was protected by the open stock law then in effect, and was free to roam. You had to fence such animals out if you could, and if they got hurt on your property, you were liable for damages. It made owning livestock a business with intriguing possibilities for profit.

I couldn't keep The Brain out of our yard or the Feinsteins', but to hasten his departure each time I made a stout slingshot. One had served me well on our farm as a varmint chaser, and the mule was a much better target than a rat or a fox. He continued to open our gates and visit, but he kept his eyes open and if he saw me with the slingshot in my hand he tore out. At first he paid less heed to Pat, but he was surprised one day to have her bang a pebble off his bony flank with the weapon, and after that he approved of neither of us. She had learned slingshot technique when she became impatient with the blue jays, for every time we got a new feeder up we got more jays. "And I can chase that hawk with it, too," she said. A sparrow hawk swooped down now and then after the cardinals we were attracting, and my wife couldn't bear it. She had taken a motherly attitude toward the birds we fed, and there was no use to tell her about the balance of nature. She thought nature a poor manager.

It was at this time that I went shopping for some less expensive bird feed, having noticed cookies and peanut butter ap-

pearing on the feeders along with the almonds. I had no wish to find myself shelling crabmeat and shrimp for the flock, as I suspected the Gentrys of doing. "How about buying some corn for these birds of yours?" I asked Pat. "Chickens like it."

She felt it rather common fare for songbirds but agreed to try a little. We stopped at a feed store and made a discovery. "Gamecock feed," Pat said, pointing to a sack. It was an assortment of small grains and priced quite a bit below the goodies the birds were currently getting. We brought home a modest sample and sprinkled it on the feeders. By that time we had twenty-one if you counted some wooden salad bowls nailed to trees. The feeders were carefully spaced around the house, however. Pat did not want Mrs. Gentry to know the extent of the competition.

The gamecock feed was an instant success. Apparently nobody else around there had tried it, and birds were fools for novelty. But what pleased my wife most was the first appearance in our yard of quail. She had never lured them before, although we had seen the covey parading through the Gentry yard almost every day. And they were Mr. Gentry's pride and joy; at heart as well as by birth he was a landed aristocrat. On seeing the quail come, Pat decided that gamecock feed was a wonder and she ordered a hundred-pound sack at once.

This was all very well, but when she spied Mrs. Gentry hurrying through the gateway between our yards the following day in a state of agitation, she almost ran and hid under the bed. "I'll bet she's coming to say we stole their quail," she gasped. But not so. Mrs. Gentry was coming not to complain but to borrow. She needed an extra pound of coffee.

"Oh, dear. Maybelle just phoned," she said breathlessly, referring to one of their friends in Pass Christian, "and she's bringing some out-of-town visitors. I suppose they want to see the bayou, and you know how *that* is, Pat. I'll have to serve something and right between shoppings, when I'm out of practically everything."

Pat loaned her a pound of coffee and was so relieved that she also pressed a plate of Danish pastries on her to see her through the visitation. Fortunately the quail were not in our yard at the moment, and Mrs. Gentry was too worked up to go around counting our feeders, either. She rushed back home with her coffee, and Pat rushed along to give her a hand before the visitors arrived.

My wife was gone half an hour or so, and during it the feed-store truck delivered our hundred pounds of gamecock feed. I was loading up all the feeders with it just to show I was a good kid, when she came scuttling back home. "Stop!" she cried in a hoarse whisper.

It seemed an odd request. Already the birds were whizzing down on the feeders I had serviced, and I had supposed this was what she wanted. But she shook her head hard.

"The Gentrys' visitor's visitors just arrived," she whispered, "and they didn't come to see the bayou—they came to see the *birds*. They're some of these terribly dedicated bird watchers, with notebooks and everything, for pity sakes. They're all lined up now on the Gentrys' gallery as solemn as toads, waiting to bird watch. And the birds are all over here."

"Maybe we'd better invite the bird watchers over here, too, then," I said, but Pat said this was socially impossible.

"I feel awful about it," she said. "I didn't mean to spoil the Gentrys' party, and I realize now that they must have an enormous reputation for keeping a bird sanctuary. We'll just have to empty all our feeders. Hurry up."

I retraced my steps, unloading the feeders I had just filled, to shrill chirps of indignation from the mob of birds. "Hope they don't keep that racket up all afternoon," I said. "They've got my ear pans thumping."

"Bird sounds are perfectly lovely," she said.

"Even the great horned owl?"

"He's interesting, at least," she said. There were several of these howlers in the vicinity. When they got tuned up after dark they made a noise that sounded something like a highway collision: "Karow! Wow-wow-wow. Ska—REEEE." It gave Mrs. Feinstein bad dreams, and I had a theory it was the original rebel yell. Pat liked it.

However, the birds did not keep up their protest when I had the feeders all bare again. I suddenly noticed it was blessedly quiet. Mysterious but welcome, I thought. I started to mention it to Pat, but she had suddenly remembered something else.

"The quail!" she said. "We want them to go over to the Gentrys' yard today. You know how they are about *them*." She hurried over and opened the fence gate. I didn't think a closed gate made any difference to quail, but she didn't want to take a chance. "And I think we'd better lay a little trail of the gamecock feed to lead them right to it," she said, and did so.

"Won't that attract the other birds back here again?" I asked, but she thought not.

"They all seem to have gone away," she said. "I don't hear a single chirp. Well, I guess they're mad but I can't help it. Now let's go in the house so we don't scare the quail off."

We went inside and busied ourselves with non-bird activities, until the phone rang. Pat answered, and it was Mrs. Gentry calling from next door. "Pat?" she said, *sotto voce*. "Have you got the birds over there?"

"I don't think so," Pat said. "Haven't you got them?"

"All we've got is a squirrel," Mrs. Gentry whispered. "And all these—these *people* lined up on the gallery in their horn-rimmed glasses, waiting."

"Well, I'll look," Pat said, "but I really don't think there's a single bird here, Mrs. Gentry."

She hung up and went to look, and she was right. There

wasn't a single bird in sight in our yard. But there was something else. "Phmff!" Pat cried. "That mule's here again."

Sure enough, The Brain was with us. Seeing no one about, he had entered our driveway gate and sauntered in. And having entered, he had found a pleasant surprise—the trail of gamecock feed laid for the quail. He was now happily munching his way toward the opened fence gate.

"He's making straight for the Gentrys' yard," Pat gasped. "And they've just got their gardenia bushes grown out again."

"To say nothing of the visiting bird watchers. In a minute they're all going to be mule watchers."

"I should never have left that gate open," she said. "Do you think you could possibly head him off?"

"No," I said, but I hurried toward the side door of the house to try. I was just sneaking out when the mule suddenly stopped eating and jumped straight up. As he did so, he opened his jaws and uttered a high-pitched "HEE-E-E-E-E!" Coming down, he executed a quarter-turn and fled back to our driveway gate and out. I slipped back into the house.

"Did you see that?" Pat cried. She had in one hand the slingshot and she was just returning from the gallery.

"What did you hit him with, for Lord's sake?" I asked. "A fireball?"

"I used the weight from my little pressure cooker." It was a heavy chunk of steel that set on the steam-release valve. "But what I meant was—did you see that perfectly enormous *bird*? It flew out of a tree when the mule jumped. It flew right across the Gentrys' house."

"Hope the bird watchers spotted it," I said as she dashed off for the bird book. "One is better than none."

It was even better than that. Mr. and Mrs. Gentry both hurried over to our yard as soon as their company left, shortly after. Mr. Gentry was more excited than I had ever known him to be. "A Cooper's hawk, by Jove," he was murmuring.

Pat, who was hovering between an eagle and a pelican identification, caught her breath. Sparrow hawks were bad enough.

"Naturally we didn't have any birds with a hawk around —everybody understood that," Mrs. Gentry said triumphantly, caressing Kyrie who was great friends with her. "I was never so glad to see anything in my life."

Mr. Gentry looked at me. "Most baffling, though," he said. "Did you hear the cry?"

"I don't think I did," I said. "How do they sound?"

"Ordinarily, hawks make a sort of wail when flying," he said, shaking his head. "But this cry— By Jove." He threw back his head. "Hee-e-e-e," he said.

I coughed. "Something just occurred to me. I wonder if it could have been the mockingbird, sir? Mocking something, you know? A . . . mule, or something?"

Pat edged delicately away from me, toward Mrs. Gentry who was discovering a couple of our bird feeders hidden in an oleander bush, aided by the traitor Kyrie pointing them out.

"Our mocker?" Mr. Gentry said, blinking. "And with a hawk about?"

Mrs. Gentry, who had just searched out three more bird feeders, concealed behind liveoaks, and was starting off around the house with Kyrie, counting on her fingers, was suddenly nabbed by Pat. "Come on," she cried. "I've got a present for you."

"Oh, lovely," said Mrs. Gentry, who would drop anything for a present. "What is it?"

"Gamecock feed," Pat said. "The birds adore it. And I think we owe something nice to the mockingbird, anyway."

We found out later that the mockingbirds had no use for gamecock feed, and Mrs. Gentry had to buy some pistachios for them. Those they ate, shrieking at Mr. Gentry to hurry up with the shelling.

16

A RACCOON SOAP OPERA

I<small>N AN EFFORT TO KEEP ITS AUDIENCE OF HOME-</small>makers from stampeding en masse to television, a radio station in Gulfport sprang a personal-service program while we were living in our house on the bayou. The program's director called it The Kozy Korner. One of its side effects was to get me tangled up with a pet raccoon for a brief while, though not brief enough to suit either of us. The raccoon was named Jack.

When The Kozy Korner program started, nothing was said about raccoons. Pat tuned it in because she was sampling all manner of odd things to capture the flavor of a new locale. She quoted The Kozy Korner announcer to me:

"This is *your* program, folks. You got something you want to buy, sell, swap—you phone me, you hear? No commercial establishments, please."

Those who responded were then heard telephoning their business to the man as if they were present in the studio, their remarks punctuated by beeps from the recording device. It was as interesting as a party line, Pat said. Most of those calling at first had something to sell: two night lamps for twenty-five cents each . . . a forty-dollar phonograph on which the caller's daughter, said to be a good Christian girl, had played only sacred music and would now sell for twenty dollars so she could buy a wrist watch . . . a bed board for $3.50 . . . some seven-week-old Pomeranian pups, fifty dollars each. . . .

The pups were priced out of The Kozy Korner market, but they started something. The calls offering twenty-inch girls' bicycles, ten dollars, and wine-colored ladies' coats used only twice, were now interspersed with appeals to help find pets on the loose. For a few days parakeets monopolized this classification. The air over the coast that season must have been dark with stray parakeets answering to such names as Billie, Twinkie, and Boo-Boo. Or more likely keeping mum, because nobody reported any luck.

"Now somebody's lost a monkey," Pat soon reported. She was not doing any business with The Kozy Korner but she found it perfectly fascinating to listen to each day. The customer who reported the escaped monkey was the wife of an airman at Keesler Field, Biloxi, and she never did find the monkey. "But," she told the announcer later, "we've met so many interesting people who thought they saw him."

It was, as you can see, a sympathetic community, ripe for pathos, and at this point it began to get it from a pair of gifted amateurs. They were twin boys, twelve years old, identified as Bobby and Billy, and they telephoned The Kozy Korner to report a missing raccoon. "His name is Rusty," said Bobby with a catch in his voice, "and he's been gone two days."

The Kozy Korner maestro, a kindly coffee-drinking man known to his listeners as Phil, responded warmly. "I'm sure we can find your pet raccoon for you, sonny," he said, apparently feeling that this one was going to be a cinch. "How would you describe him?"

"He looks kind of worried," Bobby said after a moment's thought.

"He eats bread," said Billy, who seemed to be sharing the phone, Pat told me.

"Oh," Phil said. "Well, there can't be many loose pet raccoons around. I mean." He took the boys' telephone number and address and urged them to call back the next day and let him know what happened.

They did. Nothing had happened, but the boys were not fainthearted. They had been talking it over and had decided to offer a reward for the raccoon's return. "We'll give our flashlight," Bobby said.

"With batteries," Billy the kibitzer added.

Phil seemed embarrassed at this, and so did my wife, who was following developments closely. "The poor kids," she said. "A thing like this can warp a child's outlook on life."

However, the boys appeared to know their public pretty well. The offer of the flashlight produced results. When Bobby went on The Kozy Korner air the next day, he reported that a man had shown up at their home, leading a raccoon.

"Wonderful," Phil cried, taking a gulp of coffee (you could hear him swallowing, Pat said) and sounding terribly relieved. "Then everything's turned out all—"

"It was the wrong 'coon," said Bobby.

"It wasn't Rusty," said Billy.

"Oh," said Phil, sounding as if someone had kicked his chair out from under.

"We'd like awful much to get him back," Bobby said, "and we'll give our air rifle to whoever brings him. Both our air rifle and flashlight."

"Well, gee," Phil said. "I don't— Well, all right if you want to, boys. I'm *sure* we're going to find your raccoon. We're bound to."

Phil was so exercised, he threw in a special announcement on the lost raccoon and repeated it twice during the remainder of the program. Anyone tuning in on The Kozy Korner for the first time might have assumed it was something sponsored by the Wildlife Commission.

The air-rifle-flashlight offer stirred up business in the raccoon market. The next we heard from the twins (two days

later, for they skipped a day, and Pat thought it was all over)
a total of six more raccoons had been carried, led, or dragged
to them for inspection. But none of the six was the missing
Rusty, his masters reported faithfully to Phil. I began to feel
more sorry for him than for the boys. When he got the news
his voice seemed to crack, Pat said. The boys, however, were
bearing up wonderfully and were even acquiring better mi-
crophone presence. They spoke clearly and to the point, I
was told, and their voices had none of the southern accent
which often made other patrons of the program a little hard
for the midwestern ear to understand.

The boys now seemed to feel success was just around the
corner. Indeed, judging from the comments Phil was getting
on the air, the entire listening public was looking for Rusty.
And though it already seemed excessive, the boys again raised
the reward ante. "We'll give our *bicycle* to whoever finds him
for us," Bobby announced.

Phil was too touched to answer at once. He gulped huskily,
and Bobby—or perhaps Billy—added that it was a real good
bike and that Rusty's finder would get the air rifle and flashlight too, as promised. Phil muttered that he would do his
level best, but Pat thought he sounded beat.

It was at this juncture we discovered The Kozy Korner had
an unexpected fan. He was a retired Army colonel who lived
down the road, a blunt and outdoorsy man full of energy and
not much given to such sport as The Kozy Korner offered, I
had thought. His name was Clanahan, and shortly after the
close of the program on which the boys had offered to sacrifice their bicycle, Colonel Clanahan came stamping up our
driveway looking upset.

He asked if I had been listening to that damn program,
that raccoon business, and I said I knew about it. But that
I hadn't known he—

"Threw their bike into the kitty," the colonel rumbled. "The poor little bastards. One 'coon's just the same as another damn 'coon anyway."

I said I supposed so. I didn't know much about 'coons. In fact, nothing.

"Well, I do," Colonel Clanahan said, "and I know they'll never lay eyes on that 'coon of theirs again. He's run off to the piney woods to find a mate. Gone native."

"They may still get him back if he hasn't left the state," I said. "They've got people beating the bushes from here to Hattiesburg, I judge."

"The Lord looks after children and drunkards," said the colonel, "but this is too much to ask."

Apparently it was. Even with the incentive of the bicycle the community was running out of raccoons, and only four more were brought to light. None was Rusty, the twins advised Phil, and they added their box camera to the fabulous reward offer.

At this, Colonel Clanahan paid me another visit. He sounded exasperated. "Those crazy kids must think somebody *stole* their 'coon," he said.

"Well, by now it'd pay him to bring it back," I said. "Flashlight, air rifle, bicycle, camera—that ought to be enough to get a horse back."

The colonel snorted. "Too damn much. It's ridiculous. He'd get suspicious. You can *buy* a 'coon for a couple of dollars." He surveyed me. "If you're not doing anything special, what do you say we find those boys a 'coon and put a stop to this foolishness?"

"What good would it do? They've already turned down every—"

"I'll explain the facts of life to 'em," the colonel said shortly. "They've got to learn sometime. And this way, they can keep all their toys."

We set out in the colonel's car, a jalopy he used for fishing trips, and headed for the pecan-grove country that fringed the coast. He seemed calmly confident we could find somebody with a pet raccoon to sell, and after we had drawn a few blanks at farmhouses, along with searching looks for, I supposed, our guardian, we picked up a lead.

"Fellow name of Lasser got a 'coon up the road a piece," a man informed us. "Can't say if he's for sale. Lasser raised him from a pup."

The countryside was thick with Lassers. We bounced from one to the other, seeking out the raccoon Lasser, and by the time we found him he was probably well alerted. In fact, his telephone was ringing as we drove in, and we had a few minutes to observe the raccoon. It was on a chain long enough to let it pace uneasily back and forth across the back-porch banister. The house was of unpainted pine, sagging at one corner where a pier had grown discouraged.

Lasser appeared on the porch, an amiable-looking man wearing two days' growth of whiskers. "Howdy," he said, and paused on his way down the steps to caress the raccoon, which looked amazed. "You gents in the market for pulp-wood?"

"No," said Colonel Clanahan, an unsubtle type. "We're looking for a 'coon. You want to sell that one?"

Lasser looked as if he had asked for one of the children, whom we could hear whooping in the woods near by. "Well, now," he said, exploring his whiskers with one hand. "This 'coon here's kind of a pet—"

"Want to sell him?" the colonel barked in his barracks-inspection tone.

"I don't rightly know . . ." said Lasser, and Colonel Clanahan got back into the jalopy.

"Country's full of 'coons," he grunted, kicking the starter.

"Five dollars!" Lasser yelled, and the colonel got out again.

"Throw in the chain and collar," he said, dragging out his

billfold. Looking deeply depressed, perhaps because he hadn't asked ten, Lasser chained the raccoon in the back seat of the car.

The colonel remembered something as we drove off. "What's his name?" he thundered back.

"We call him Jack," Lasser yelled.

"Appropriate," the colonel muttered as the raccoon climbed onto the back of the front seat and peered anxiously over our shoulders. "He cost enough of it."

We drove back toward the beach, with the raccoon breathing down our necks and fingering our shirt collars as if he was a small clothing merchant examining the fabric. "No use wasting time," Colonel Clanahan said. "Let's deliver him. What's those kids' address?"

I felt as if I had heard it from Pat a hundred times but I hadn't memorized it or their telephone number.

"We'll stop by the radio station," the colonel said with authority. "That Phil fellow ought to know."

Phil knew the address by heart. He would probably know it to his dying day. He came running out to the car when the studio receptionist in the little cottage-type station called him for us, and he leaned in, gazing at the raccoon. "So that's him," he said heavily. "Thank God. Those kids—" He stopped. "This one *is* Rusty, isn't it?"

"He'll do," said the colonel. "This is a better 'coon than the one they lost. This one's got a collar and chain."

Phil sighed. "Would you mind letting me know?" he asked. I said we'd be happy to, and we drove off to the address he had given us and which I now recalled perfectly. It was that of one of the nice homes on the beach road, and as Colonel Clanahan tooled his fishing jalopy up the wide semicircular drive, a yard man gave us a weary, hopeless stare, and a well-dressed matron sitting on the front gallery looked startled. The colonel got out of the car and bowed smartly.

"Colonel Clanahan, ma'am," he said. His manner was courtly in a military way, and the lady didn't happen to notice the raccoon in the front seat. She relaxed visibly. "Are Bobby and Billy around, ma'am?" the colonel asked. "We've got a little present for them."

"My grandsons?" the lady said. "Why, how nice of you, Colonel. They're visiting me this summer, as I suppose you know, and they're just now back from a swim, right back here—" She started to escort him to the grounds behind the big house, but the colonel, remembering the delicate educational aspect of his mission, interrupted.

"We'd like to surprise them, ma'am," he said firmly. "It's about that radio thing, you know."

"Radio?" The lady looked vague. "Well, I've been away for a week on some urgent family matters, so I haven't . . . Well, you'll find them around back, Colonel."

We drove around. The boys were shucking off their swim trunks in a summerhouse; an intelligent-looking pair of kids, I thought. On the skinny side but tanned. They emerged bright-eyed, wriggling into shorts and T-shirts, and spotted the raccoon in the car at once.

"Which one's Bobby?" the colonel asked. Bobby held up a hand, and the colonel captured and shook it in a manly fashion. "I'm Colonel Clanahan," he said, "and I've brought you—"

"That one isn't Rusty," both boys said together as if someone had pressed a button.

"I know it isn't," the colonel said just as promptly. The boys looked startled. "His name's Jack," added the colonel, "and he's a mighty fine 'coon. As fine a 'coon as you'll find, and I want to explain some things."

"But he isn't Rusty," Bobby said.

"We just want Rusty back," said Billy. They looked at each other in a downcast way, and the colonel hunched his shoulders impatiently.

"Now you boys listen to me," he said. "You've got to face this thing like little soldiers. This is part of growing up, understand?"

The boys looked bewildered.

"A 'coon's like anything else," the colonel said. "Just like a man. When the time comes, he wants to . . . I mean it's his nature to look up . . . He gets to feeling . . ." He stopped. Both boys were looking at him with great interest, and the colonel ground his teeth.

"He wants to raise a family, dammit," he said.

The boys nodded and waited hopefully, but Colonel Clanahan seemed to feel he had now made sex crystal clear. "So there you are," he said, dusting his hands together. "It was that time. How old was Rusty?"

The boys spoke together. "Two," said Bobby as Billy said "Five."

Colonel Clanahan blinked.

"I . . . meant two," Billy murmured. "I forgot. Sir."

Colonel Clanahan came to parade rest and looked hard at the twins.

"I think Grandmother wants us now," Bobby said, edging away.

The colonel, with muscular co-ordination that would have done credit to a master sergeant, shot out his hands and seized both by the napes of their T-shirts. His eyes slowly swept the grounds. "Where," he said steadily, "is that bicycle you were offering to give away?" The boys, in the grip of iron, gazed at each other.

"It's . . . around," Bobby said feebly. The colonel gave him a little shake. "At home," Bobby croaked.

"Home where?"

"C-Columbus, Ohio," Billy mumbled.

"And the air rifle? And the flashlight? And the camera?" demanded the colonel, spacing his sentences as the district attorney might have.

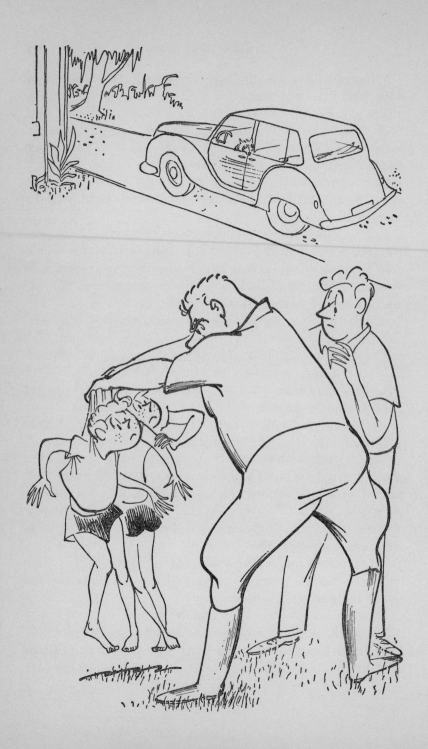

"The camera . . . we brought along," Bobby whispered in a bottom-of-the-well voice.

The colonel let go of them and folded his arms. "You boys—" he said with terrible deliberation, "you boys never *lost* a 'coon. *Did* you?" There was no answer. "You boys never *had* a 'coon," said the voice of outrage. "*Did* you?"

The boys looked at each other from the corners of their eyes. "Well," Billy said, rubbing one leg against the other, "once we *knew* somebody that had one. In Colum—"

Colonel Clanahan made a terrible noise deep in his throat. His face grew eggplant-colored and the muscles in his shoulders bunched as he grabbed. But the boys were keeping their eyes on him this time and they leaped out of reach, though not an instant too soon. The colonel, his hands snatching air, bellowed out a few remarks that must have snapped up heads all over the neighborhood. Then he swung around and dumped himself back into his car, still rumbling and fizzing.

"Get that goddam 'coon off my neck," he said as we rolled out. "It's full of fleas."

I chivvied the raccoon. "Maybe we should have left it with them, Colonel."

"I wouldn't even leave the fleas with 'em. Little shysters."

"Still," I said as we drove home, "they did make quite a show on the air. They'll probably grow up into a remarkable pair of promoters. I'm almost sorry now that the thing's all over."

"Isn't quite over," said the colonel, sounding calmer. "You still have to call that Phil fellow."

"I just meant that one of us would."

"You're the one," said the colonel. "I wash my hands of the whole thing. I'm going fishing."

We set the raccoon free when we got home, and after a few incredulous moments he hurried up a liveoak and out of Colonel Clanahan's life. He did not quite leave mine until the next

day. I put off calling Phil until then and might not have remembered it at all except that I found myself scratching,
which brought the raccoon sharply to mind.

My wife seemed to be busy, so I went to the telephone without bothering her about it and called the radio station. Phil
himself answered, which suited me fine. I was anxious to wash
my own hands of this fiasco without dragging anybody else
in on the conversation.

"About those kids and the raccoon," I said as soon as Phil
spoke.

"Yes, yes," he said. "The lost raccoon. Rusty. Bobby and
Billy's pet."

He doesn't have to fill me in, I thought, after the time I
wasted on this business yesterday, but I assumed it was oc-
cupational habit. "Well, they didn't lose any raccoon," I said.

"D-didn't— What did you say?" Phil asked, and I could hear
him gulping a hasty swig of his coffee.

"I said they didn't lose it." There was a blank silence broken
only by a beep. "They didn't even *have* any damn raccoon,"
I said, raising my voice. "Can you hear me all right? The
joke's on us, Phil. We were all suckers for a couple of little
slickers, get it?" I had to laugh, thinking of how the kids had
fooled everybody into scurrying around to help find a raccoon
that never was. "Haw, haw," I said. "These smart little
phonies have been pulling everybody's leg. I don't know how
in hell they ever got the—"

There was a gurgly noise. I got the peculiar idea that Phil
had just lost his swig of coffee. "Beep!" went the phone again.

"What's this beep thing?" I said. There was no answer.
"Say," I said, "are you recording this silly conver—"

My wife rushed around the corner. "Oh, my goodness," she
said. "You just went off the air."

I hung up quickly. "Off the *air?*"

"You were on the program."

"That Kozy Korner thing? It's that time?"

She nodded, her eyes wide. "I was listening. I had no idea—"

I groaned. "Dammit, why didn't he tell me?"

"You started talking right off. He didn't get a chance." She looked at me, biting her lip. "I wonder if they'll do anything to you? Of course you didn't know. But isn't there a law about language on the air?"

I didn't care to think about it. I scratched myself and started for the bathroom. "I'm going to take a bath. A great big bath. And if anybody calls, you haven't seen me lately."

She began to giggle. "You know, you sounded pretty good on the air. Especially when you got violent. I was standing there listening, thinking I'd sort of like to know that man, and then all at once I thought: Good heavens—I do!"

17

THE $1000 GOLDFISH

NE DAY AFTER WE HAD BEEN LIVING IN THE house on Bayou Portage for a while, Pat and I made the mistake of taking a drive upcountry a piece. We didn't go far, just three miles, but it was too far. "Stop—there's a house for sale," Pat cried.

"We've got a house," I said and would have sped by, but she made as if to grab the steering wheel. I turned in and stopped before the drive gate, a tumbledown wreck.

"The place is vacant," Pat said. "Let's go look." Women, I knew, could not pass a vacant house. I had followed my wife through hundreds of them, occasionally at times when a five-dollar down payment would have bankrupted me. However, she didn't want to buy most of the places, and to tell the truth, I liked to poke around them too.

We climbed over the gate, which was padlocked, and Pat raced around the front yard clapping her hands over the planting. It was impressive. Orange trees, kumquats, quinces, pomegranates; a magnolia, several papershell pecans, Oriental persimmons; some huge old azaleas, camphor trees galore, and around the house, a small cottage, were fig trees. Wisteria climbed high into the tall pines along with Cherokee rose vines, and just then the sweet olive was blooming, two great tall bushes of it, almost trees, perfuming the air with a fresh-fruit fragrance.

There were three acres of grounds surrounded by a heavy

hedgerow. The plot was triangular with the house setting at about the middle point. Behind it to the north was a nice pinewoods, and the south acre in front was an old run-down pear orchard. Just west of the house a jungle of bamboo that had got out of hand was trying to take the place. Pat inhaled the scented air ecstatically. "Let's see if we can get inside," she said. "I'm dying to see this little place."

We walked up the front porch steps. They were rough, though sound enough—concrete—but the porch floor was a ruin, the boards patched here and there with old automobile license plates. And the front door was locked. Pat looked into a window through cobwebs. She was looking into the living room and could see into the kitchen beyond. She was fascinated, and when I teetered around to the other end of the L-shaped porch and found that someone had broken a window, she reasoned that this gave us a perfect right to go in. "To see what damage they did, the trespassers," she said.

I opened the window and we climbed into the living room. It had a few pieces of furniture and was about fifteen feet wide by twenty long with an offset on one end. "I'd change that doorway and put it around the corner," Pat said. The doorway she meant opened into an adjoining bedroom and was to the right of a small brick fireplace which backed up to another one in the bedroom.

"Don't get too interested," I said as we stepped into the bedroom, a small one, and had a look at the bathroom, which was a drab old thing.

"Do you know," she murmured, "we've never had a bedroom with a fireplace." I steered her toward the bedroom doorway again, and she hurried out to the kitchen. It had a slant ceiling following the roof line and a great deal of storage and work space. A strip of little windows looked out on the woods. The floor here was of concrete, showing the kitchen had been added to the original dwelling, which had a single wood floor.

"We could do something with this place," she said.

I was glad Kyrie wasn't along with us that day. She would have howled in pain if she knew what Pat was saying. The house was far from her idea of the life beautiful. For one thing, walls and ceilings in living room and bedroom were covered with a water-stained brownish paperboard half an inch thick and in random widths, probably Army surplus. "What could you ever do with that, for instance?" I asked Pat.

She made airy motions. "Paint it white. It'd look just like wood paneling." At the moment it looked just like blotting paper, a point I recalled with deep feeling later on when I started buying paint for it. Because we did buy the place. Not immediately, though.

"What do you think it's worth?" Pat asked. "Just for instance?"

"It isn't on water. And it's run down badly."

"But charming," she said.

"Hasn't got any heating system, either, except the fireplaces. In fact, it hasn't even got gas, not even bottled gas."

"But the grounds are bursting with fruit and flowers," she said.

I looked at the ceiling. "Roof probably leaks, too. And I imagine termites are all through the timbers. If you hear something cracking, run for the window."

"I asked you what it was worth, not what's wrong with it."

"I might go to twenty-five hundred," I said, and she threw up her hands. We took the address of the real estate man from the sign and went to his office in Pass Christian. The asking price was $8,500, and while I was cranking up to dash right out again, he said he thought $6,500 would buy it.

"That's just crazy," Pat said, and I beamed at her. "Why, it's a run-down wreck," she said. "It isn't on water and it hasn't got a furnace and the roof leaks and it's full of termites."

The real estate man patted his brow. "I don't think the roof leaks, ma'am," he said mildly. "It might have a few termites, but they haven't chewed it down in twenty-five years. If you'd like to make an offer, I'll forward it. Owner's a lady in Florida."

We offered $4,000, a figure I had come up and Pat down to, and a week later the owner refused it with an aggrieved air. We had thought she would but in the meantime we had put our bayou house on the market and had driven out to see Pear Orchard, as we were calling it for convenience, a few times.

These trips had given Pat an even more possessive air toward the little place, and she was concerned about the way the azaleas needed water. I was brooding over the orange and fig trees. The house had stood vacant for five or six months and it was a wonder things looked as good as they did, for the soil was sandy.

But when our offer was refused, we promised each other we'd forget all about the place. For by now we both desired to live at Pear Orchard and fix it up, overruling Kyrie. As I had thought, she took the view that nobody in his right mind would care to live there, though she was willing to visit.

We were getting a lot of lookers at our bayou house, though no takers as yet, when one day we drove past Pear Orchard and saw somebody else looking over the gate. They intended to snap it up at once, we had no doubt. Folly seized us, and we made another offer—$5,500—and it was accepted.

Like our bayou house, Pear Orchard got its water from a flowing artesian well. And, also like the other one, the well was on someone else's property. This did not disturb us at first. It was a common enough arrangement. Water ran slowly from a faucet in the yard where we could fill buckets and water the plantings. This we did for several weeks, and then the flow became less. We were in a dry-weather cycle and the whole gulf coast had been growing, so that there were more people using more water and lowering all artesian pressures. When, finally, it took ten minutes to fill a single bucket, we decided to pay a visit to the well itself. It belonged to a family named Meadowgate, and Pat was curious about their place anyway. The house stood well back from a road-side grove of big magnolias, and from what we could see through the leaves it was an ante-bellum plantation type.

We drove into the side lane leading to it and I hit the brake pedal. The Meadowgate car was rolling grandly out the drive, a big black Rolls-Royce sedan.

It stopped, its huge headlights glaring at the invading rabble. The Meadowgate heir, a man in his thirties and wearing a beret, was driving. "Tell him we want to see that well," Pat said.

"Do you know what that is?" I whispered. "That's a Rolls-Royce."

"I'd as soon ride in a hearse," she said. "Ask him what's happened to the water."

I got out and introduced myself as the new owner of the little place across the road.

"Charmed to know you," said Mr. Meadowgate. "Trust you're comfortable."

"We aren't living there yet," I said, "but the water—"

"Ah, the water," he said, waving one hand about. "Splendid water, what? Comes from our well, you know."

"So I understand," I said. "But not very much."

"Quite," said Mr. Meadowgate pleasantly. "Flow's down. Lovely weather, isn't it?"

"Lovely, lovely," I said. "So we were wondering if the well—"

"Artesian, you know," he said, shifting gears. "No pump, please."

"We don't have a pump," I said, "but it looks as if—"

"Water rights restricted to free flow only," he said. "Wish you happiness of the place, old man. Charming spot."

I returned to our car and backed out of the lane. "Hey," Pat said. "We were going to find out what's wrong with that well."

"Quite simple, old dear," I said. "Charming flow's gone down. Lovely luck, what?"

On a hunch I borrowed a Stillson wrench from our open-handed bayou neighbor Feinstein, took it out to Pear Orchard and removed the two-foot vertical pipe on the outside faucet. Immediately water gushed out, filling the hole I had dug to get at the connecting ell. I enlarged the hole into a thirty-gallon pool, and Pat, who had small faith in my plumbing, changed her mind. Now we could dip water to succor wilting plants. But presently the pool raised another problem. We suspected mosquitoes were breeding there, and in a foolish moment I did something about it, or thought I did. I bought three goldfish for nineteen cents each in a dime store in Gulfport, hoping they would devour mosquito larvae in the pool.

"They're kind of cute," Pat said, watching them swim about the little pool. "Let's name them."

We didn't know boy fish from girl fish so we dodged it by naming the biggest Gulfport, the next biggest Biloxi, and the littlest fish Pass Christian.

As if in appreciation for the honor, a Gulfport real estate firm showed up at our bayou house shortly after with a bona fide customer in tow.

"Quick," Pat cried. "Now we have to remodel Pear Orchard so we can move in." We had a month to do it in.

We had spent too much remodeling the bayou house. We planned to do Pear Orchard on a shoestring and we started with a secondhand one. A neighbor down the road decided to sell a small building he had been keeping bee supplies in. We made sure the bees had left, and bought it for $100. We had it moved intact, knocked one wall out, and joined it on that side to the bedroom. This required making a doorway out of one of the bedroom windows, but we thought we now had two bedrooms, until it dawned on us that the only way to get into a bed in the tiny beehouse would be to jump in over the footboard.

"We could call it Kyrie's room, I suppose," Pat said, and Kyrie, who liked the more fashionable bayou neighborhood and had no wish to spend her declining years in such a lower-class manner, flounced out to the sagging porch.

In a way the beehouse neighbor solved the problem for us. He was so surprised at selling the beehouse that he decided to sell his garage, too. It measured twelve feet by twenty and had six nice windows. We bought it for $250 and had it hauled over and attached to the beehouse. This required us to knock another wall out of the beehouse. We then knocked out most of a third wall to put in double windows and began to wonder why we had bought the beehouse at all. It had dwindled into a hallway.

"We'll save something on the house painting, though," Pat said, "if you do it."

I decided to do the inside painting but to speed up the job outside I hired a local lad named Lafayette to help me. I had hired him to cut back some bamboo just before that, to make room for the additions, and was impressed by his cheerful nature. I set him to work slapping on outside white, and with a sample of the living-room wallboard in my hand, went looking for a flat white paint that would cover it in one coat. All the paint experts in Gulfport shook their heads and asked why I had ever bought such stuff, and finally one said that flat enamel might do it. I bought five gallons for a king's ransom, opened one, and set to work. The wallboard soaked it up like water. Instead of five hundred square feet to the gallon I ran dry at one hundred or less. I went after another gallon, in a shed where Lafayette and I were keeping our supplies. Expecting to find four gallons of my expensive enamel there, I found but one and while I was batting my eyes, cheerful Lafayette came in, pried off the lid and began stirring like mad.

"Lafayette!" I said. "That's *inside* paint. That's not your paint."

"Hm-m-m?" said Lafayette with a happy smile.

"Is that where those other three cans went?" I cried. "You used this expensive stuff on the *outside?*" He looked politely puzzled. I squatted beside him and pointed to the label. "See? 'Interior' it says."

Lafayette ducked his head and chuckled. "Well, that's sure a joke on me," he said. "Didn't get much schoolin', y'see." Lafayette, in fact, could not read. After that, I kept the inside paint inside where he couldn't get at it. And not counting his help the miserable wallboard in the two rooms soaked up fifteen gallons of flat enamel to achieve a passable two-coat job.

Meanwhile, carpenters were rebuilding the porch and making a bedroom-bathroom-closet suite out of the ex-garage; a plumber was putting in fixtures and a floor furnace and gas

line; and electricians were whistling about. Pat, positive we wouldn't have an untrampled bush left, kept following the workmen about, crying warnings, until they leaped in alarm even when she said hello.

"But at least we won't have to drill a well," she assured me. Though we could not put a pump on the line from the Meadowgate well, we were advised we could catch the water in an underground tank and pick it up from there with a pump to run into the house.

We went out to look at the goldfish and soothe our nerves. We stared aghast. They were floundering about in a few inches of water at the bottom of the pool. The merest trickle was coming from the pipe.

"Maybe it's just temporary," Pat said, biting her lip.

It wasn't temporary. We brought a bucket of water from the bayou house to put the goldfish in till the water should start flowing again, but the trickle had become a drip. And we were now due to move to Pear Orchard in a week.

We called in a well-driller for advice, and he advised us to drill a well. "Let's make it an artesian," Pat said. "Then we'll have water flowing into a pool for the goldfish and a little waterfall to entertain them." The driller also told us what had happened to the Meadowgate well—they had an underground gridiron of leaky pipes, and the older they got the more they leaked. "That leaves less water for you," he said.

He brought his rig, and by the time we moved he had water flowing. I dug another pool, with a little waterfall and a brick edging and at the bottom a brick castle. We dumped the fish in, and they immediately hid in the castle.

"I hope this thing isn't going to cost us too much," I muttered. We didn't have the bill yet. The cost depended on the depth.

"It's the only kind of goldfish pool I'd have," Pat said. "I like water running in but I don't want to listen to a pump going."

Then one morning she found only two goldfish in the pool and came running to me. "Biloxi's disappeared," she cried.

I thought he, or she, might be hiding in the castle but a search proved fruitless. Only the smallest and biggest fish were in the pool. We thought Biloxi may have jumped out and expired on the grass, but found no corpse.

It remained a mystery for a few days. Then Pat found another gone. "Now Gulfport is missing," she cried. I hurried to the pool. True enough, our finest specimen had vanished. Only little Pass Christian was left, swishing about in a helter-skelter manner.

"Somebody's stealing them," Pat exclaimed.

But nothing else was missing. "Would you take a chance on a skinful of buckshot just to swipe a fish?" I asked.

"I wouldn't be taking a chance. You haven't got a gun."

"I'm probably the only man in Mississippi who hasn't, but you're the only one who knows it."

"Then you tell *me* what happened," she said.

I inquired of a neighbor man who, I had noticed, also had a pool. "Raccoons," he said at once. "They're hell on fish. Doesn't your dog chase them?"

Our dog was worthless in this respect, but I didn't care to admit it. I said she was showing her age and winded quickly, which was just as true and more respectable.

"It's the raccoons," I told Pat. "Every time I get mixed up with a raccoon I lose."

"Well, don't worry," she said. "We're going to have oodles of baby fish. I just found their eggs floating in the pool." I hadn't thought our fish were mature enough to breed, but there was a mass of tiny pellets embedded in a jelly in the water.

"That's something, anyway," I said. "At least they declared a dividend before it was too late."

And then the bill for the well came in.

I stuck it in my pocket and went looking for Pat. She was

on hands and knees at the poolside. "Would you care to guess what this well—" I said.

"Look," she cried. "The little fish have hatched out. Hundreds of them."

I looked. Then I stooped down and looked closer. I grunted.

"You don't seem very pleased," she said.

"Take another look. Those aren't fish."

She bent closer to the water. "Tadpoles!"

I drew the bill from my pocket. "A thousand bucks. For that squib Pass Christian and a mess of tadpoles to have a place to swim."

We walked slowly into the house, each thinking our own thoughts.

"But we've got plenty of water," Pat said at last.

"We could have got it a lot cheaper by not going down to China for a flowing well to feed a pool."

We walked back to the new bedroom, which looked out on the fish pool. Or frog pool. "With all this water, we could dig a pond like the one on the farm, and fill it," Pat said.

"Soil's too sandy. Takes clay to hold water."

"How about a swimming pool, then?"

"We don't swim enough. And we can't afford it."

She was looking out of the window, and suddenly she grew tense. "Look," she whispered. "Taking a bath at the edge of the pool."

"All I see is a bird," I said, expecting at least a raccoon.

"It's a prothonotary warbler! We've never had one before. It's the pool that brought him, don't you see?"

"For that kind of money we ought to get a peacock."

She snatched up an old pair of opera glasses she used for bird watching and trained them on the pool. "I think I see a painted bunting coming in, too. And a cedar waxwing. Glory be."

"Call me if you see a raccoon," I said. "He'll be after a thousand-dollar goldfish for supper."

"Oh, goldfish," she said. "I'd rather have birds any time. What good are goldfish?"

"Ask our well-driller," I said, getting out my checkbook, but she wasn't listening. A tufted titmouse was dropping in for a bath, and a cardinal was considering it.

BEWARE—LION DOG LOOSE!

I N ADDITION TO ITS FRUIT TREES, PEAR OR-chard's pecans were something to drool over. Two of them were big trees and bore good crops. Unfortunately the squirrels were just as interested as we were, and they used no judgment at all. We were willing to share a few nuts with them but we took it hard that they started stripping the trees in the summertime while the nuts were still green, pitching them to the ground in disgust as fast as they pulled them off. Kyrie was a little help at first in making the squirrels less bold but she was growing old and her eyesight was declining. Then one sad day in her twelfth year her heart failed, and she died in my arms.

"The thing to do is to get another dog at once," we were advised by a tenderhearted friend who had rushed us an emergency dose of digitalis pills for Kyrie in her last hours. We were too distressed for the time being to want any other dog. But after a week had passed we missed Kyrie so much that we changed our minds. And this raised a problem. We were planning to leave Mississippi, and now that we had no dog, the move would be so greatly simplified that we hesitated to own another until we were resettled.

"Maybe we could borrow a dog," Pat said after we had talked it over without coming to any decision. She mentioned the friend who had brought the digitalis and who had several old cocker spaniels of her own. "I'm almost sure she'd loan us one of her female cockers," Pat said.

"Before we say anything to her," I said, "I think we ought to mention it to Colonel and Mrs. Randolph." They were friends who bred Rhodesian ridgeback lion dogs. They had once offered to give us one of their male dogs but we had backed off for three reasons: we really preferred females; we didn't think another female would get along with Kyrie; and since the lion dogs were priced at three hundred dollars, we felt it was too expensive a gift. "But since they once offered us Copper," I said, the name of the male, "I think they'd appreciate our telling them what we're planning to do."

I phoned and got Mrs. Randolph, a vigorous and forthright woman. I told her of Kyrie's passing and that we were planning to borrow a dog for a while until we sold our place. "I don't want you to think we don't like Copper, Maude," I said hastily, for she was starting to speak up, "but a female dog—"

"Do you want to borrow one of our bitches, Ken?" Maude cried.

I hadn't realized they had a spare one. "Well, that's awfully kind of—" I said.

"You can borrow any of them," Maude said. "We aren't breeding right now and we'd be glad for any of our dogs to stay with you. I'll go talk to Frank."

"Well, thanks, Maude," I said. "I— Maude? Hello—?"

I returned to Pat. "Maude wants to loan us a bitch."

"Watch your language," Pat said, and suddenly opened her eyes wide. "What? Did you say they want to loan us—a lady lion dog?"

"They aren't breeding them right now. I think we ought to be flattered."

She bit her lip. "Don't those lion dogs seem pretty fierce to you?"

I didn't know a great deal about them except that they had originated in Africa where they were bred to hunt big game, and that the "ridgeback" part of the name came from a strip of wrong-way hair up the center of the back. I had often seen the Randolph dogs, and they were compactly muscular, shorter-legged than a Doberman and shorter in the muzzle, with uncropped ears and tail. They came in varying shades of tan, or wheaten, and weighed up to ninety pounds. And they were decidedly cool toward strangers.

"I guess they're fierce," I said, "but I wouldn't mind having one around for a while just to see what they're like."

The Randolphs arrived in their station wagon shortly after, with the lion dog. "This is Patti—" the colonel said, and a tan blur rocketed out of the wagon, made a fast rounding of the house, and rose to her hind legs under one of the pecan trees, glaring silently upward. The squirrels up there chattered in fright. They had got used to Kyrie, who hadn't walked on two legs very often and who had given them a sporting chance by barking.

"She seems to chase things all right," Pat murmured.

"Don't worry," Maude Randolph said. "She'll chase everything in sight."

"Are there any special instructions?" I asked Colonel Randolph. "Feeding and so on?"

"Quite simple, Kenny boy," he said. "Feed her ordinary dry chow in the evening."

"Easy enough," I said. "Just like Kyrie."

"Yes indeed," he said. "And at about ten in the morning she gets her tea."

"I beg your pardon?" I said.

"Orange pekoe will do nicely. Rather weak, with plenty of milk. No sugar."

"She drinks that?" I said.

He nodded. "Improves the coat. Gives it tone. Old African custom."

I had never given Kyrie tea in her life. I wondered if Patti relished coffee too, and perhaps brandy and a cigar after dinner.

"Oh, and I made you a list of the official commands," the colonel said, pulling it from his pocket.

I reached for it. "That'll be quite a help—" I stared at the list. "*Kjoo?*"

"Means 'come,'" said Colonel Randolph. "Swahili, you know."

"We have to talk to her in *Swahili?*"

"Quite simple," he said. He raised his voice. "*Kjoo,*" he yelled. Patti looked over her shoulder and wagged her tail. She returned her attention to the squirrels.

I consulted the list again. "*Keti?*"

"Means 'sit,'" he said.

"*Lala?*"

"Lie."

"*Tulia?*"

"Means 'quiet.'"

"*Maji? Chakula? Kaa?*"

"'Water,' 'food,' and 'stay.' Nothing to it, you see."

"Does she know any English?" I asked.

"We like to be consistent," he said. "Her sire and dam are both champions, both whelped in Rhodesia."

When they left, Patti raced after their car, inside our fence, to the end of the orchard. "I think I'll change her name," Pat said, gazing after her. "'Patti' sounds so much like 'Pat' that people will think I'm being cutie."

"I'm afraid you'll have to live with it," I said. "I wouldn't dare change anything. You don't realize what a fancy beast this is. Have we got any tea in the house?" She peered at me. "Patti has tea at ten of the morning," I said. "Polishes her hide or something."

"You'd better call her back before she tears her hide on those thorns in the hedgerow."

I consulted my list. "*Kjoo,*" I yelled.

"Gesundheit," Pat said.

"That's Swahili for 'come.'"

"Swahili!" She put her hands on her hips, and I nodded. "Well," she said, "I don't see her coming."

I roared it out again. Patti was smelling a pear tree. She seemed to be deaf. Pat marched up the orchard. "Patti!" she cried. "You come right back here." Patti gave her a brief glance and continued about her smelling.

"You see?" I said. "Doesn't understand a word of English. You have to use Swahili."

Pat selected a fallen pear branch and advanced on Patti, brandishing it. "You get right back to the house," she said. "*Get.*" Our borrowed lion dog missed me by inches on her way back to the house. "Swahili," Pat said to me, flinging away her persuader.

"Maybe you ought to feed her," she said a while later, after Patti had danced around the pecan trees some more and had terrorized redbirds and towees by not only chasing them off the feeders but leaping into the air after them as they bugged out. "I think she's trying to catch herself a dinner."

I started after a half bag of chow left from Kyrie's stores and then recalled something I wanted to do first. "I want to weigh her on an empty stomach," I said. I had always weighed Kyrie by picking her up in my arms like a sack of turnips, weighing both of us and then subtracting my own weight. I brought the bathroom scale outside and started to heft Patti. Her teeth closed on my left ear, and I let go so fast she fell down. "Some other time," I said, feeling to see if my ear was still all there.

She ate a hearty dinner out of Kyrie's old bowl but absolutely refused to use Kyrie's cushion when we brought her inside. "*Keti,*" I said, consulting my list. Patti smelled my feet. "*Lala,*" I said sternly. She wagged her powerful tail, sweeping a couple of ash trays off the coffee table behind her.

"Oh, for heaven's sake," Pat cried, fetching broom and dustpan. "Sit," she bawled. Patti sat. "That's the trouble with dogs with tails," Pat said. "She'd better just lie down, it's safer. You lie down." Patti lay down on the floor. "Was that some more Swahili you were saying to her?" I nodded. "What does it mean?" Pat asked.

"We were just chatting," I said, refolding the list.

We got her some newspapers to lie on, since she preferred them to the cushion, and passed a calm evening except for once when she fell asleep, had a bad dream, and leaped to her feet with a volley of barks that stood our hair up.

The phone rang as we were about to go to bed. It was Colonel Randolph, to see how things were going. Going fine, I said. "Did she eat all right? Does she seem to feel at home?" he inquired. I told him everything was rosy.

"Oh—one thing," I said. "She won't use Kyrie's cushion, but we're bedding her down on newspapers in the living room. Okay?"

"The living room?" Colonel Randolph asked.

"Yes. We're going to keep her inside, just like Kyrie," I said, fingering my chewed ear and feeling it was pretty big of me, considering.

"She's used to sleeping in the bedroom," said the colonel.

"We've only got one bedroom," I said, "and Pat and I are using it."

"She sleeps at the foot of your bed," he said. "It's characteristic of the breed. They insist on being with their people. All the time."

As I hung up Pat was on her way to the bedroom. She was sort of skating, hanging onto Patti's tail and screeching at her to come back. "She sleeps in the bedroom," I said as they passed me, headed for the bedroom.

"Not in my bedroom," Pat shrieked back. I followed. Patti

was trying to lie down at the foot of the bed, my wife batting her with a pillow. I explained about the characteristic of the breed. "Characteristic my foot," Pat said. "I'm not going to be kept awake all night listening to her dreams. Get her out of here."

I got her out with a bribe of suet, and she spent the night in the living room, dividing her time among marching around, growling at the windows, and gnawing the door that barred her from our company.

When Pat saw the door the next morning she wanted to take a broom to Patti and have an understanding. Kyrie had never eaten the woodwork. I advised patience but we couldn't take too long to reach an understanding with Patti—we were putting the house on the market and we didn't want it gnawed down. In fact we were just about to spruce it up.

"Instead of closing the door tonight," I said, "I'll put a couple of chairs there."

This didn't work very well. As we retired to the bedroom that evening, Patti's face, all furrowed with worry, peeked after us through the chair rungs, and ten minutes later there was a fearful clatter. We rushed out and found her with her head caught in the rungs of one chair, backing around the living room trying to shake loose.

Another ash tray bit the dust, as did a floor lamp, and then she happened to back into the big brass wood bucket at the fireplace. The racket it made in tumbling evidently reminded her of some terrifying experience from puppy days. It frightened her and gave us an idea. I disconnected her from the chair and placed the bucket in the doorway. It worked beautifully. She refused to squeeze by it and didn't try to jump over, and we all went to bed again.

Since she had her bluff in on the squirrels, we felt now that we were fixed. I got in touch with a carpenter who lived down

the road, and a painter next door to him, and asked them to
drop by the next day and spend it on the sprucing up so we
could start the real estate man to work on selling the place.
Meanwhile, Pat was studying the habits of our lend-lease lion
dog.

"Maude Randolph was certainly right," she said. "This dog
chases everything. Now that the squirrels have stopped coming around so much, she's branching out."

"Chasing birds some more?"

"Not only birds. She dived into the pool and tried to catch
Pass Christian. And then rabbits, and now lizards."

We encouraged lizards, which ate bugs. "How many has
she caught?" I asked anxiously.

"She can't catch them. She just chases—" She stopped short.
Outside our gate someone was honking a horn with an expensive three-note sound.

"Probably the carpenter or painter," I said. "Business must
be good."

"Ha," said Pat. "I know who that is. It's that Bible woman
back. You go talk to her this time."

We had never had Bible salesmen call on us until we moved
to Mississippi, but there they made regular rounds. The salesmen were women and when you opened the gate they put a
foot in and said firmly, "I'd like to discuss the Bible with you."
We already owned two or three Bibles, but they weren't selling Bibles—they were peddling an obscure magazine on reli-
gion. It took about ten minutes to worm this out and another
fifteen to pry them loose.

"You go," I said to Pat. "I don't have time."

"I'm busy," she said, starting to pull weeds in a flower bed.
"You go."

Neither of us had to go. Patti went. She came racing from
the orchard where she had been chasing lizards up the pear
trees, and hit the gate a tremendous thump with her front
paws. It was a solid board gate we had had built, seven feet

high, so Patti couldn't see what was on the other side. Nor could the Bible woman see Patti. "Hello?" we heard her saying in a loud, strained voice. "Who's there?"

Our lion dog accommodated her. She crouched and suddenly sprang straight up into the breeze like a cat—or a lioness, perhaps, for she looked something like one in the face. Her great tawny head appeared momentarily, glaring over the tall gate, and from outside it there came a piercing screech. I hurried to the gate and opened it, holding Patti by the collar, but the Bible salesman was already on her way, charging down the road in her car, horn blaring and order blanks flying out the windows as if it was Mardi Gras.

"We'd better put a sign on that gate," Pat said, "to warn people."

"BAD DOG?"

"That's kind of an insult to the dog. Maybe BEWARE OF LION DOG."

I painted a sign and added an improvement. "See? BEWARE —LION DOG LOOSE!" I said. "So they won't think she's tied up." I nailed it on the gate and it had an immediate effect. The carpenter I had called came by to start work and left without even getting out of his car. So did the painter.

"I don't want no truck with no loose *lion* dog," said the carpenter when I looked him up. "Regular dogs are bad enough." The painter seconded the motion.

"Aw, fellows," I said. "That sign doesn't mean you. I'll keep her in the house while you're there."

"Ain't that the one that chaws through doors?" the carpenter said. "And run off the Bible lady? No sir."

I saw that the neighborhood grapevine had been working, too. I gave up and brought home my own lumber and paint. I could do a passable job myself in a week.

"You're going to do it yourself?" Pat cried when I appeared and explained the situation. "Oh, my sainted aunt."

"It's just patching and touch-up," I said. "Don't act as if you married the village house wrecker."

"I mean it'll take you so long. Heavens—you've only got two days." I gaped at her. "I just called Mr. Clancy," she said. He was the real estate man. "He's coming out day after tomorrow with a prospect," she cried.

We had picked Clancy to sell Pear Orchard because he was such a live wire but I hadn't expected him to start sparkling so quickly. I made haste to get on with the job, trying to think of any short cuts I could get by with before Clancy arrived. I thought of several and was already through patching some decayed framing and flooring on the porch when Clancy phoned back.

"What's this I'm hearing about you having a *lion* dog out there?" he asked Pat. "Is there such a thing?"

She assured him there was.

"Well, I don't know, then," said Clancy. "I don't go for dogs. Bad for business to have a vicious dog. Customers get the idea the neighborhood's—"

"She isn't vicious!" Pat said.

"How's she act with strangers?" Clancy asked darkly.

Pat consulted her conscience and compromised with it. "She hasn't quite met any strangers here yet," she said carefully. "But she's a very highly pedigreed—"

"I'll think it over," Clancy muttered. "It's a long trip out to get bit."

Pat reported the conversation to me. I was now on a ladder with a can of white paint, touching up some of the places my carefree helper Lafayette had used inside paint on. "I couldn't lie to him," Pat said. "Besides, I didn't know how much he'd heard. And we *don't* know how she acts with strangers."

"I've got a pretty good notion," I said. "But I'll call Clancy back this evening when I'm finished painting. He's sold a lot more property out this way lately than anybody else, and I don't want to lose him."

I worked till dark and planned to call Clancy at his home right after dinner when he was feeling mellow. But as we were starting on our own dinner we noticed a persistent honking coming down the road. The car it was coming from stopped outside our gate and the honking continued. Patti sprang to the living-room window and barked savagely. "It's the bootlegger," I said to Pat.

She cupped a hand to her ear. "What?"

"*The bootlegger*," I said, drowning Patti out.

"Oh, darn. This is his night, isn't it?" She glanced at Patti roaring at the window. "Slip out the back door," she said. "I'll keep her inside."

I got my wallet, turned on the front-yard floodlight, and slipped out without Patti's noticing. The bootlegger was a friendly man named Possett, and I had met him originally through our neighbor Feinstein on Bayou Portage. Mr. Feinstein had bought some lumber from Possett and then discovered his sideline. I had sampled Possett's moonshine there and after I got my breath back had declined with thanks. It was cheap enough—five dollars a gallon—but gasoline was cheaper and legal and tasted about the same. We became friends anyway, and I kept an eye thereafter on reports of still-raids in the *Daily Herald* to see if Possett had landed in the jailhouse.

I had another reason for doing so. When Possett couldn't sell me liquor, he had offered to sell me fresh eggs. Besides his sawmill he had a small farm in the piney woods and his eggs were much better than those at the store. I was glad to buy them and the only drawback was his delivery time. He brought them when he made his bootleg rounds, after dark. He was nice about it, though, and carried them on the seat

of the car, not tucked around the engine under the hood
where he transported the moonshine.

"Hiya," he said when I admitted him and closed the big
gate securely behind his car. "Wha's all the barkin'?" Patti
was continuing her uproar in the house, though Pat had
closed the window almost all the way to discourage her.

"Just the dog," I said, not wanting to get involved in telling
him all about Kyrie's recent death. Possett had liked Kyrie
and he was such a sentimental man that I was afraid the
news would upset him and delay things. He was slow-moving
at best, and I couldn't understand how he always outran the
muscular young Alcohol Tax Unit boys. Every time he came
by, they had just chased him through the woods again lately,
according to him. "Lost mah cooker again las' week," he'd
say, laughing merrily. The things were made of copper and
cost him $175 each, he told me, and I thought he had quite
a sense of humor.

He was now gazing pensively toward the house, but when
I made no move to get Kyrie, as he thought, to greet him, he
opened the trunk of his old Ford. "Brought y' a present," he
said, and shyly lifted a burlap sack of potatoes out. "Frash
dug."

I was touched and pleased. We liked new potatoes and
hadn't had any good ones since we were raising our own on
the farm. Possett's gifts were usually medicine bottles filled
with a nauseating anise-flavored liqueur he made, which he
occasionally brought under the impression Pat doted on it.
I never had the heart to tell him she used it to kill fire ants.

I took the sack gratefully and staggered back toward the
garage to stow it while he got the eggs.

My panting did not quite mask a hideous sound of splintering from the front porch as I got to the garage. There was no
barking but I had no doubt it was Patti the lion dog. It was.
Though Pat had closed to within three inches of the sill the
window she was barking at, Patti had suddenly shoved it up

with her strong muzzle when she saw Possett handing me the
sack. She probably thought he was attacking me, and she had
wriggled through onto the porch. The screen door was no
problem to her. She had gone through its middle bracing as
if it wasn't there.

I dropped the potatoes and raced back, sure that Patti
was accomplishing in a few moments what the Alcohol Tax
Unit had been trying to do for thirty years. I yelled her name
as I went, though paying heed had not seemed one of her
strong points, but when I made it back I was stunned to find
Possett unhurt and, on the whole, charmed. He was holding
the bag of eggs, and Patti was glaring at him with what
Colonel Randolph called beautiful amber eyes and which I
considered mean yellow ones. But she wasn't attacking—just
rigidly holding a guard pose.

"Ah thought this's Kyrie," Possett said, chuckling. "Tha's a
joke on me."

He showed not the slightest fear, so I introduced them and
said Kyrie wasn't there just now, and changed the subject.

He left, waving cheerfully to Patti and me, and we returned to the house by way of the ruptured screen door. Pat,
who had been in the kitchen keeping dinner warm when the
ruckus occurred, was in a state. "Did she bite him?" she
gasped. "I was afraid to go see."

"She just guarded him," I said. "We've been worrying for
nothing. She only goes after things that run away from her."

Pat put her hands on her hips. "Well, I like that!" she said,
regarding Patti hotly.

"You mean you wanted her to chase him?"

"She could have chased him a little bit. Just for appearances."

I was satisfied the way it was. Patti was more sensible than
I had given her credit for. And now I could call Clancy with
a clear conscience and tell him he was safe. I went to the
phone, in the beehouse hallway to the bedroom, and started

to dial his number. As I was doing so I was hit an appalling blow at knee level from behind and I sat on the floor, the telephone following, as Patti boiled past.

"What the hell's wrong with her?" I bawled, scrambling up as Pat arrived around the corner. "She acts as if she smelled a lion, dammit."

"Sic 'im," Pat cried to Patti. "That's a good girl!" She turned to me, apologetically. "I'm sorry she ran into you, but she and I were after it and I guess she didn't see you. She was looking at the floor."

"After what, for Lord's sake?" I said, trying my knees.

"Oh. A spider," said my wife. "It turns out she's very good at chasing them, too. I couldn't be more pleased—it will help with the housework, and I'll want to keep the place looking extra nice now that it's on the market."

Selling Pear Orchard turned out to be quite a job since it was too far from town for a good many people and didn't have the lure of being on water. However, the interval gave us time to get well acquainted with our visiting lion dog—so much so that Pat's conscience bothered her when at last Clancy showed up with a purchaser, and we prepared to leave.

"Patti thinks she's our dog now," Pat said. "I'm afraid it'll break her up when she finds we aren't taking her." Patti was eying our packing with suspicion and I, too, wondered how she was going to take the desertion that was coming. I need not have concerned myself. I had forgotten for the moment how pets had always regarded me.

When Colonel Randolph came to reclaim Patti, she knew instantly what he was there for. She leaped into his station wagon—a thing she had never done on his frequent visits before that—and took root in the front seat, gazing straight ahead into the glorious future. "Be a good girl," I said through the window.

"Everything will be all right, Patti," said Pat beside me, biting her lip. Patti gave us a pleasant twitch of one ear, and when the colonel climbed in, she buzzed her tail and slobbered all over him.

"I guess . . . she'll be all right," Pat murmured as we watched them drive off.

I tried not to smile, for Pat seemed to have a lump in her throat. "Yes, she'll be all right," I said. "It's your reward for marrying me, honey. It's catching. You can worry with me for the birds and the beasts, but they'll never have frets over you."